Daily Prayers
❧ for Busy People ❧

Daily Prayers
❧ for Busy People ❧

by William J. O'Malley, SJ

Saint Mary's Press
Christian Brothers Publications
Winona, Minnesota

This book is for
Tom Kenny, SJ,
and
Rita Rose

The scriptural text throughout this book is freely adapted. These adaptations are not to be interpreted or used as official translations of the Scriptures.

The publishing team included Carl Koch, FSC, development editor; Mary Duerson Kraemer, copy editor; Holly Storkel, production editor and typesetter; Evy Abrahamson, illustrator; pre-press, printing, and binding by the graphics division of Saint Mary's Press.

The acknowledgments continue on page 186.

Printed in the United States of America

Printing: 6 5

Year: 1996 95 94 93

ISBN 0-88489-242-5 perfect bound
0-88489-248-4 spiral

 # Contents

 # Introduction

Why I Wrote These Prayers

In the twenty-five years since I was ordained a priest, I never found the breviary much help in reminding me who I really am. Instead, praying the breviary became a routine, obligatory, and barren chore to be gotten out of the way of my real jobs. It was, for one thing, too long. For another it was—quite frankly—boring. I felt hard put to find a single prayer or hymn in it capable of moving the human mind or heart or spirit. And the bulk of the breviary, the psalms, was clotted with Zalmunnas, Epaphras, and Sebas, which meant nothing whatever to me, no matter what they might mean to scholars. In all those years, I never once took time to look up the meaning of those "horns" the unrighteous were tirelessly brandishing in the psalms.

More importantly, I found the psalmists too often waspish and vindictive. For instance, Psalm 109 curses, "May their children be homeless vagabonds and hounded from their lands." To pick out precise individuals to whom I wouldn't mind that happening was too tempting for whatever is unredeemed in me. Many of the psalms, at least to my mind, justified and ritualized precisely what Jesus had forbidden: "You have heard you must love your neighbor and hate your enemy. But I tell you: love your enemies and pray for those who torment you" (Matthew 5:43–44).

Thus, this book evolved. Each time for prayer is very brief, but I suspect one psalm is better than no psalm at all. Nor are the psalms in this book translations. Rather, they (and other scriptural readings) are free adaptations. The hymns are not relics esteemed primarily for their age and orthodoxy but poems written by men and women adept at making words touch the human soul. The prayers attempt to focus the unclarities of my own daily life and the lives of those who have brought their confusions to me.

These prayers merely open a small place a few times a
day for God. After that, I have found, God has a way of
taking over the whole field from me, which, of course, puts
God and me precisely where we ought to be.

God can pop in front of our face at any time, like a falling star suddenly searing quicksilver across a night sky. In
moments that James Joyce called "epiphanies," the God
who lurks under the surface of everything can suddenly
burn through the skins of things and transfigure them, grip
us in awe, undeniably present: in a mountain peak at sunrise, a giggling infant, a heart-stopping phrase in a book, a
painting so "right" that we are hypnotically frozen before
it. Those are the numinous, privileged moments—the
"Oh, my God" moments. And "Oh, my God," of course, is
precisely the appropriate response—because that is just
whom we have encountered.

These moments do not occur every day, nor do they
occur to those whose souls are inaccessibly swaddled in the
iron bands of dull routine, souls on the defensive at nearly
every turn, against the boss, the competition, or the kids. If
we are always wary of "them," we will also be wary of God.
We may be quite sure of one thing: God is always very
polite and will never intrude if we are too busy.

In the Gospels, Jesus says that the Master will return
when we are least ready, like a thief in the night. At the
time, he was talking about death—or about the end of the
world, but God's visitations are not always that dramatic
or terminal. Essentially, Jesus enjoined us to be vigilant
and receptive, like Mary at the Annunciation. A homely
analogy perhaps, but we have to be as ready for God as
parents are when they say, "Come anytime. Your room's
always ready." Their waiting is not demanding but serene,
not nervous because God does not show up in a blaze.
"Come anytime."

Using still another homely analogy, what this book
attempts to be is a series of setting-up exercises, to keep us
limber, open, centered, ready, but content merely to be in
God's presence, out of space and time and the hurly-burly
for awhile. At peace. We should rid ourselves of the old
foolishness that prayer should be a time of "saying prayers."
Prayer is merely being vulnerable to God, being with God.
And if God does on occasion flash out and leave us feeling

ravished and awed, that is of God's choosing. Remember Mary's words, "Behold the handmaid of God, be it done to me according to your word" (Luke 1:38). Not mine.

Making Time and Creating Space

For a long time, I believed that I did not have enough time for prayer, what with classes to teach, papers and preparations, plays to direct, writing, counseling, and games to attend. My list of alibis would make you weep, as I am sure yours would too. I consoled myself with the rationalization that to work is to pray. There is a sure truth to that, though in my case it was bald self-deception. The work I did in the name of God had become an idol, so had the school, the kids, their parents, and the applause.

Suddenly God dealt me a heart-bruising blow, the kind that brought me to my knees—which is, perhaps, the best place from which to see who we truly are and who God truly is. For days, I couldn't *not* pray, even if most of it was imploring that "this chalice pass from me," trying to change God's mind. Then, when God's mind proved unchangeable, nothing was left but to go on, which required first healing that God-inflicted wound. Slowly and softly I could hear God moving around in the back rooms of my soul and urging me: "Let go. I'll catch you." And I did. And God did.

Since that dark time, I know that there is always time for God, no matter how cluttered and chaotic my day gets. There must be time. Not for God's sake. For mine.

Take a worst-case scenario. No matter what we claim, we who are traveling salespeople, lawyers, or teachers can always find a half-hour or at least fifteen minutes to pull off the road and stare into the God-drenched space. For harried working parents, finding moments is harder. But the busier we are, the more we need to withdraw awhile to remind ourselves of what is important, to keep our heads straight and pointing in the right direction. At the very least, praying three times a day reminds us that we do not have to be perfect, that we are not the be-all and end-all. Somebody Else has all those jobs.

We should ask ourselves: Is maintaining a relationship with God as important as a coffee break? As important as reading the newspaper? We need not give up coffee or the paper, but if God is a genuine priority in our life, a couple of things do not really have to be done "today or else."

Choosing a place to pray is of some importance too. Of course, we can pray on the subway or the bus, but it often takes industrial-strength concentration, though any prayer at all is better than none. Experimenting with places can be fun, I have found. Our school chapel was too small for me, though someone else would find it cozy and just right. My room had too many ungraded papers and the telephone. So the best place turned out to be outside while I was walking back to the dorm to change clothes after school. No handbook shows how to choose a place or a time. The only important issue is the decision to go in quest of them.

Suggestions for Using These Prayers

The prayers in this book are divided by days, but these are merely handy divisions. There is no need to finish any of the prayers. The book is like a matchmaker. If God suddenly shows up, lay the book aside as you would if any other guest arrived.

The most important element of prayer is placing ourselves in God's presence. Whatever way we pray, a conscious shifting of gears or pulling out of the rat race into the Timeless is crucial. Simply rolling a mantra over and over in our mind is far different from rolling the mantra over within a keen awareness of God. Prayer begins with being connected to God. One way I find helpful to remind myself of the ever-present God is to say over and over again, "God, my great friend, . . . somehow you're alive in me." At times, I am sure, you will need nothing more than that. But the essential difference between thinking and praying is the conscious "connection."

The goal of these prayers is connecting with and resting in God, not trying to learn anything or to make "progress in the spiritual life." Remember, God will lead us as God will, and God's faithfulness, goodness, and love for us are infinite.

Praying Communally

Although these prayers were composed primarily for personal use, they may be used communally. The prayer leader should invite other people to read passages. Allow some time for silent meditation between passages. Prayers are not races. Take time in God's presence.

When gathering for communal prayer, people need sufficient space in which to feel comfortable, receptive—not apprehensive, not ready to take charge, but open, ready, and centered.

If members of the group feel edgy about praying together, invite them to close their eyes and relax their body, letting all tension, all being-in-charge, all deadlines, the need to perform, drain out of their face, shoulders, back, arms, and legs. For these few moments, the world can get along without them.

When the group has had a chance to relax, help them slow down their breathing. Suggest that they take long and deep breaths and exhale slowly. A period of meditative breathing in God's presence is a prayer of simple attention. Minor as it seems, this deceleration is as essential as deciding to pray. Unless we slow down, we cannot pull off the road. As people breathe deeply, read the Presence prayer (found at the beginning of each prayer time) and remain silent. Let God do the work. If you are leading the group, you, too, have to be aware of being too much in charge.

As Adam and Eve, Abraham and Sarah, Moses and Peter discovered, the most difficult surrender in the world is to let God be God. These prayers call us into God's presence, provide a way of connecting to God, and invite us to surrender to God's care.

❧ First Week ❧

First Sunday

MORNING

Presence

Living God,
you dwell in the inmost silence of my soul.
Open me,
inward to you,
outward to those I meet today.
Keep me aware of your presence and power in me.
Help me to infect everyone I encounter today
with freedom and joy.

Grace: Jesus, that I may see.

Psalm 8

Oh God, my God.
How utterly your presence fills all the earth!
The stars sing your glory back and forth across the night
    sky.
You have made the wide-eyed children and their wonder
to be your great surprise
for the learned,
for the sophisticated,
for the world-weary.
When I look up at the vast heavens,
at the stars you fashioned with your fingers
and set spinning through endless space and time,
I stand in wonder of you.
What is humankind
that you care so for us,
that in this steady and loyal universe
you chose such changeable creatures as us?
You made us only a little less than yourself.
You have crowned us with glory and honor.
You have taken all that your hands have made
and given us rule over it—
darkness and light
waters and sky,

plants and trees and their seed,
fish, birds, beasts,
because, of all your creatures,
only we are made in your image.
What is humankind, that you care so much for us?
Oh, God. My God!
How utterly your presence fills all the earth!

Hymn

The world is charged with the grandeur of God.
    It will flame out, like shining from shook foil;
    It gathers to a greatness, like the ooze of oil
Crushed. Why do men then now not reck his rod?
Generations have trod, have trod, have trod;
    And all is seared with trade; bleared, smeared with toil;
    And wears man's smudge and shares man's smell: the soil
Is bare now, nor can foot feel, being shod.

And for all this, nature is never spent;
    There lives the dearest freshness deep down things;
And though the last lights off the black West went
    Oh, morning, at the brown brink eastward, springs—
Because the Holy Ghost over the bent
    World broods with warm breast and with ah! bright
        wings!
        (Gerard Manley Hopkins, "God's Grandeur")

Offering

God, my friend,
I offer you this day.
Let all my prayer, work, joy, suffering today
join with the lives offered to you
by the whole People of God
and especially with our great Eucharist,
Jesus,
your Son and our Brother.
Let your Spirit be with me today,
especially in . . .
And I ask your loving concern today,
especially for my friend . . .
Remind me, through the day, that I am not alone.
Amen.

DAYTIME

Presence | Living God,
at the stillpoint
wherein my frailty falls into
your forevermore
and intersects,
let your forgiveness flow through me,
out to those
who deserve it least.

Grace: Abba, forgive them. They know not what they do.

Psalm 51 | God, my great friend,
crush my vindictiveness and set me free of it,
so that you can infuse joy in its place.
Don't let me wall out your presence and your Spirit
with vengefulness and spite.
Save me from my weaker self.
Help me not to close myself round my petty grudges.
Keep my spirit open
to those whose weaknesses differ from mine
only in kind.
Instead, I will teach the wayward
the way to you.
I will bring my fellow sinners home.

Hymn | The quality of mercy is not strained,
It droppeth as the gentle rain from heaven
Upon the place beneath: it is twice blessed;
It blesseth him that gives and him that takes:
'Tis mightiest in the mightiest; it becomes
The throned monarch better than his crown;
His scepter shows the force of temporal power,
The attribute to awe and majesty,
Wherein doth sit the dread and fear of kings,
But mercy is above this sceptered sway,
It is enthroned in the hearts of kings,
It is an attribute to God himself,
And earthly power doth then show likest God's
When mercy seasons justice.

              (William Shakespeare, *The Merchant of Venice*)

"I hope, my lords, in the divine goodness and mercy, that as Saint Paul and Saint Stephen, whom he persecuted, are now friends in paradise, so we—differing in this world, shall be united in perfect charity in the other. And I pray God to protect the King, and give him good counsel."
(Thomas More, adapted from E. E. Reynolds,
The Trial of St. Thomas More)

The scribes and Pharisees brought a woman to Jesus. She had been caught in adultery. They stood her up in the middle of the onlookers and said to him, "This woman here was caught in the act of adultery. In the Law, Moses ordered that a woman like this ought to be stoned to death. What do you have to say about that?"

Silently, Jesus bent over and started writing in the dirt with his finger. The officials weren't to be put off and kept pushing him to answer. Finally, Jesus looked up at them from under his calm brows. "Whichever of you has never sinned, let him be the one to come forward and throw the first stone at this woman."

When he bent over and began to write on the ground again, they waited for a while, but then, one by one, starting from the oldest, they drifted silently away. Finally, Jesus sat there alone, with the woman standing sadly in front of him.

He looked up from the ground and asked, "Where did they all go? No one left to condemn you?"

"No one, sir," she said.

"Then, neither do I condemn you," Jesus smiled. "Go now. Try not to sin again."

(John 8:3–11)

God of kindness,
most of the days of my life
I have asked you to forgive my trespasses against you,
but only insofar as I forgive
those who trespass against me.
Remind me of my need
to be forgiven
and to forgive.
Amen.

EVENING

Presence

Living God,
my spirit is overshadowed and quickened
by your Spirit,
asking to conceive your Son within me.
Be it done unto me as you will.

Grace: Living God, not my will but your will be done.

Psalm 104

Dreamer of the universe, you set the earth spinning
in the cold silence of space.
You raised up the land and made it fertile,
where the beasts by darkness
and ourselves by the light of day
can claim our food from you.
The grass you made to serve the beasts of the field,
and the beasts to serve us,
and us to serve you.
May I offer you, freely,
the acceptance of the yoke
all creatures have
written in the fibers of their being.
You never cease renewing the world.
Renew me.

Hymn

       More servants wait on Man,
Then he'l take notice of: in ev'ry path
      He treads down that which doth befriend him,
      When sicknesse makes him pale and wan.
Oh mightie love! Man is one world, and hath
       Another to attend him.

      Since then, my God, thou hast
So brave a Palace built; O dwell in it,
      That it may dwell with thee at last!
      Till then, afford us so much wit;
That, as the world serves us, we may serve thee,
       And both thy servants be.

                     (George Herbert, "Man")

Holy Friend,
accept this day as the best I could return
for what you've given me.
Forgive my slips along the way,
and remind me to begin to heal them tomorrow.
Till then, let me leave the world awhile to you,
in peace, to sleep, to heal myself,
and to wake to serve you yet again.
Amen.

Closing

First Monday

Presence | Living God,
somehow, you're alive in me.
Help me to give that aliveness away.
Weaken the defenses I protect myself with—
against the boorish, the cynical, the demanding,
and against the healing that can come through me from you.
Let my vulnerability to their aggressiveness
give them pause.

Grace: Jesus, I believe. Help my unbelief.

Psalm 11 | I take shelter out in the open,
in the hands of my creator.
My friends tell me, "Fool, be cautious!
The sly have their arrows already notched,
ready to shoot the honorable from the shadows."
But the world I dwell in
is the temple of my maker,
whose presence is everywhere,
even beneath the most unlikely masks,
even within the wicked.
Their punishment is being unaware of God,
crouching inside the heat of their anger,
the cold of their emptiness.
It is the honorable who see God's face—
everywhere.

Hymn | Batter my heart, three person'd God; for, you
As yet but knocke, breathe, shine, and seeke to mend;
That I may rise, and stand, o'erthrow mee, and bend
Your force, to breake, blowe, burn and make me new.
I, like an usurpt towne, to'another due,
Labour to'admit you, but Oh, to no end,
Reason, your viceroy in mee, mee should defend,

18

But is captiv'd, and proves weake or untrue.
Yet dearely'I love you, 'and would be loved faine,
But am betroth'd unto your enemie;
Divorce mee, 'untie, or breake that knot againe,
Take mee to you, imprison mee, for I
Except you'enthrall mee, never shall be free,
Nor ever chast, except you ravish mee.

                (John Donne, Holy Sonnet 14)

Prayer

Friend,
you can make miracles with most unpromising means—
a universe from nothing,
a nation from withered Abraham and Sarah,
the mother of our Savior from a simple country girl.
I offer myself,
with all my impairments and imperfections.
Make miracles with me.
Amen.

Offering

God, my friend,
I offer you this day.
Let all my prayer, work, joy, suffering today
join with the lives offered to you
by the whole People of God,
and especially with our great Eucharist,
Jesus,
your Son and our Brother.
Let your Spirit be with me today,
especially in . . .
And I ask your loving concern today,
especially for my friend . . .
Remind me, through the day, that I am not alone.
Amen.

🌿

DAYTIME

Presence

Living God,
I tell you nothing when I say that I am wounded.
You gave me hollow spaces inside,
to remind me what I am.
There are hurts within me left by others,
daring me to trust again—and yet again.

And there are wounds I've brought upon myself.
But here I am.

Grace: Jesus, by your wounds we are healed.

Psalm 146

Living God,
I offer you my life, a song of praise,
disjointed and at times, perhaps, off-key.
I yearn to place my trust in those around me,
and I'll try,
because you ask it of me.
But never call it easy.
You trusted Peter, Judas, and the rest.
You know.
But you are the one forever faithful, if too slow.
You vindicate my fumbling to be honest,
my search for truth,
my halfhearted struggle to be free.
You shock my blindness with your light.
You wrench my crooked stumbling straight.
You lure me from the quicksand
with all your voices saying, "Please . . . ?"
When I cry out, "Enough! No more!"
lead on.

Hymn

When, in disgrace with fortune and men's eyes,
I all alone beweep my outcast state,
And trouble deaf heaven with my bootless cries,
And look upon myself, and curse my fate,
Wishing me like to one more rich in hope,
Featured like him, like him with friends possessed,
Desiring this man's art and that man's scope,
With what I most enjoy contented least;
Yet in these thoughts myself almost despising,
Haply I think on thee—and then my state,
Like to the lark at break of day arising
From sullen earth, sings hymns at heaven's gate;
For thy sweet love rememb'red such wealth brings
That then I scorn to change my state with kings.

(William Shakespeare, Sonnet 29)

Brothers, be not afraid of men's sins. Love man even in his sin, for that already bears the semblance of divine love and is the highest love on earth. Love all God's creation, the whole of it and every grain of sand. Love every leaf, every ray of God's light! Love the animals, love the plants, love everything. If you love everything, you will perceive the divine mystery in things.

> (Fyodor Dostoyevsky, *The Brothers Karamazov*)

Reading

I saw God enthroned in the sanctuary, surrounded by fiery presences, humbled, exultant, and ready. And they shouted to one another as one voice: "Holy! Holy! Holiest is the God of all ministering spirits whose presence quickens all that is!"

Their voices trembled the foundations, and the house brimmed with the cloud which veils and reveals God's presence.

I moaned, "I haven't the slightest hope! I'm doomed. I stand before the Morning, and I'm but a ghost of incompleteness, one of unclean heart, from a people of unclean hearts, and I've looked on Yahweh Sabaoth."

Then one of the fiery ones flew to me, holding a blazing coal from the Presence in a pair of tongs. He burned it into my lips and whispered, "See! God's presence purges you. Your impurity is gone. You are whole."

Then I heard the voice of God: "Whom shall I send? Who will go for us?"

And I heard my own voice say: "Here! Send me."

> (Isaiah 6:1–9)

Scriptural Reading

God of power,
you made my emptiness so you could fill it.
Beethoven was deaf,
Homer and Milton blind,
Lautrec crippled.
Use my woundedness.
Send me.
Amen.

Closing

EVENING

Presence | Living God,
Catch me up.
Slow me down.
Abide with me.

Grace: Holy Friend, let me commit my soul into your
hands.

Psalm 39 | God, my God,
once I vowed to muzzle my mouth,
lest I blame you for my weakness.
I was mute—for awhile.
But it smoldered and flared out:
"When will it come, then?
How few days have I left?
Show me how fragile I am.
You have given me only one handful of life—
a puff of wind,
a shadow.
I am the cloth;
you, the moth.
I am here only as a wayfarer,
pilgrim,
lodger.
And I grow weary."

Hymn | No! I am not Prince Hamlet, nor was meant to be;
Am an attendant lord, one that will do
To swell a progress, start a scene or two,
Advise the prince; no doubt, an easy tool,
Deferential, glad to be of use,
Politic, cautious, and meticulous;
Full of high sentence, but a bit obtuse;
At times, indeed, almost ridiculous—
Almost, at times, the Fool.

(T. S. Eliot, "The Love Song of J. Alfred Prufrock")

Holy Friend,
let me be content
with who I am.
It is the gift you've given me.
Hush me when I complain
of what I need and lack,
of when I try and fail,
of those I love and lose.
You gave me life and that's enough.
I give you back today
a small gift, to be sure,
but nothing to be scorned—
if not by you,
then not by me.
Amen.

Closing

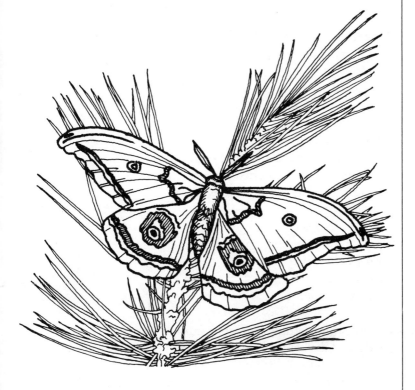

First Tuesday

MORNING

Presence

Living God,
I did nothing to earn waking today.
Others more worthy than I did not.
It is a gift I needn't have been given,
which makes today more precious.
Come into the still center of me,
so that I can be your eyes and ears,
your hands and heart
today.

Grace: Jesus, that I may have life—and have it more
abundantly.

Psalm 19

The heavens shout the holy presence of God!
One day cries it on to the next,
and night to night.
There is no sound,
and yet their songs suffuse the earth!
Above us, God has pitched the sun a tent,
and now the Son comes striding forth,
exultant,
ready for the race.
Up over the edge of earth the Morning comes
opening the day,
offering life,
summoning me.

Hymn

I caught this morning morning's minion, kingdom of daylight's dauphin, dapple-dawn-drawn Falcon,
in his riding
Of the rolling level underneath him steady air, and
striding
High there, how he rung upon the rein of wimpling wing
In his ecstasy! then off, off forth on swing,

As a skate's heel sweeps smooth on a bow-bend: the
       hurl and gliding
Rebuffed the big wind. My heart in hiding
Stirred for a bird,—the achieve of, the mastery of the
       thing!

Brute beauty and valor and act, oh, air, pride, plume, here
       Buckle! AND the fire that breaks from thee then, a
       billion
Times told lovelier, more dangerous, O my chevalier!

    No wonder of it: sheer plod makes plough down sillion
Shine, and blue-bleak embers, ah my dear,
    Fall, gall themselves, and gash gold-vermilion.
           (Gerard Manley Hopkins, "The Windhover")

Offering

God, my friend,
I offer you this day.
Let all my prayer, work, joy, suffering today
join with the lives offered to you
by the whole People of God
and especially with our great Eucharist,
Jesus,
your Son and our Brother.
Let your Spirit be with me today,
especially in . . .
And I ask your loving concern today,
especially for my friend . . .
Remind me, through the day, that I am not alone.
Amen.

🦋

DAYTIME

Presence

Living God,
open my heart,
my mind,
my hands.
All three feel more secure with some defenses.
And the price of their contentment
is my soul.

Grace: Spirit of God, set no guard upon my lips, that I
      may fearlessly proclaim your good news.

Psalm | Today, when someone begs a kindness, give
when it is in your power.
To part with freely sets you free.
Today, don't say, "Come back tomorrow,"
when you can do it now.
To part with quickly is giving twice.
Today, laugh and walk away
when the useless quarrel starts to stir.
To part in peace rises above mere winning.
Our God mirrors back our heart,
giving as we give:
the flattering lie,
the muttered curse,
the bitter mock.
Our God's favor to wise and foolish
is the same:
more of what they've chosen.

(Proverbs 3:27–35)

Hymn | "Before I built a wall I'd ask to know
What I was walling in or walling out,
And to whom I was like to give offense.
Something there is that doesn't love a wall,
That wants it down." I could say "Elves" to him,
But it's not elves exactly, and I'd rather
He said it for himself. I see him there
Bringing a stone grasped firmly by the top
In each hand, like an old-stone savage armed.
He moves in darkness as it seems to me,
Not of woods only and the shade of trees.
He will not go behind his father's saying,
And he likes having thought of it so well
He says it again, "Good fences make good neighbors."

(Robert Frost, "Mending Wall")

He came. He entered space and time and suffering. He came, like a lover. Love seeks above all intimacy, presence, togetherness. Not happiness. "Better unhappy with her than happy without her"—that is the word of a lover. He came. That is the salient fact, the towering truth, that alone keeps us from putting a bullet through our heads. He came. Job is satisfied even though the God who came gave him absolutely no answers at all to his thousand tortured questions. He did the most important thing and he gave the most important gift: himself. It is a lover's gift. Out of our tears, our waiting, our darkness, our agonized aloneness, out of our weeping and wondering, out of our cry, "My God, my God, why hast Thou forsaken me?" he came, all the way, right into that cry.

(Peter Kreeft, Making Sense Out of Suffering)

Reading

There is someone impoverished among you, one of us, in whatever town or place your creator has freely given you to grow in. Do not close your heart or hand against that heart and hand. Open yourself—heart and hand—and give enough to meet their needs. Do not be mean-spirited when the chance is at your fingertips. Do not say, "I will wait till the time is right." That time is now.

When you give, give without resentment, as the Creator gives to you, even when you are least worthy. God will bless your giving. Of course the poor will never cease coming. They are God's gift, to open us to them and to God.

I command you, then: open yourself—not just to those who have a claim on you. To anyone who asks. Anyone. Because Anyone is a disguise for God.

(Deuteronomy 15:7–11)

Scriptural Reading

God of love,
teach me to be generous,
to give and not to count the cost,
to strive and not to heed the wounds,
to labor and not to ask for rest,
to toil and not to seek reward,
except knowing that I do your will.
Amen.

Closing

EVENING

Presence

Living God,
draw me into your peace;
settle my soul;
let me take hold of today
and cede it back to you.

Grace: God, wherever I run, give me the sense to see you
already there.

Psalm 23

God of peace, you are my shepherd
You fill my every true need.
You lead me to green pastures of peace,
to the still waters of surcease,
to heal my soul.
Though the day is a dark valley
and howling shadows dog my steps,
I feel no fear.
Your crook is there to fend them off,
your staff to prod me on.
Ah, good God!
You spread a feast before me,
a food my foes are far too fierce to share.
You are my host.
You serve me
as your honored guest.
You give too much for me to hold.
Now, I see.
The shadows that pursued me
were not my foes.
They've been your goodness and your kindness,
the shadow of your hand.
Wherever you shall lead me now,
I am in your house
forever.

I fled Him, down the nights and down the days;
   I fled Him, down the arches of the years;
I fled Him, down the labyrinthine ways
   Of my own mind; and in the mist of tears
I hid from Him, and under running laughter.
      Up vistaed hopes I sped;
      And shot, precipitated,
Adown Titanic glooms of chasmed fears,
  From those strong Feet that followed, followed after.
      But with unhurrying chase,
      And unperturbed pace,
    Deliberate speed, majestic instancy,
      They beat—and a Voice beat
      More instant than the Feet—
   "All things betray thee, who betrayest Me". . . .
Halts by me that footfall:
Is my gloom, after all,
Shade of His hand, outstretched caressingly?
   "Ah, fondest, blindest, weakest,
   I am He Whom thou seekest!
Thou dravest love from thee, who dravest Me."
     (Francis Thompson, "The Hound of Heaven")

Holy Friend,
you have shadowed me today,
at my side,
sharing.
"For all that has been—Thanks!
To all that shall be—Yes!"
Amen.
     (Dag Hammarskjöld, *Markings*)

First Wednesday

Presence

Living God,
you've drawn me again from the darkness
into your light.
Kindle that light in me,
so that you and I
can begin again.

Grace: God, bid me come and see.

Psalm 40

Holy God, I waited for you.
And waited.
And finally you were there,
bending to hear my cry.
You drew me back
from the edge of the depths,
when I thought I could journey alone.
You held me, calmed me,
steadied my steps on stone.
You've turned my cry into song.
See how they gape at the joy of it!
They call me fool.
But they don't know joy,
or song,
or you.
Wonders tumble from your hands!
Such plans you have for us!
You don't want the ram,
caught by its horns in the thicket.
You want me.
So here I am.

My road calls me, lures me
    West, east, south, and north;
Most roads lead men homewards,
    My road leads me forth

To add more miles to the tally
    Of grey miles left behind,
In quest of that one beauty
    God put me here to find.
                (John Masefield, "Roadways")

Hymn

God, my friend,
I offer you this day.
Let all my prayer, work, joy, suffering today
join with the lives offered to you
by the whole People of God
and especially with our great Eucharist,
Jesus,
your Son and our Brother.
Let your Spirit be with me today,
especially in . . .
And I ask your loving concern today,
especially for my friend . . .
Remind me, through the day, that I am not alone.
Amen.

Offering

🦋

DAYTIME

Living God,
come into the still place
at the center of my emptiness,
which you hollow and hallow,
where you empower me to serve
as I could never serve alone.

Presence

Grace: God, take me in hand, and use me.

Psalm | The awesome spirit of God is upon me.
I am anointed—
opened—
enspirited!
I am sent forth
to fire the hearts of the lowly,
to heal the heavy-hearted,
to shatter the shackles of slaves,
to set the fettered free,
to announce the Amnesty of God!

(Isaiah 61:1–2)

Hymn | a man who had fallen among thieves
lay by the roadside on his back
dressed in fifteenthrate ideas
wearing a round jeer for a hat

fate per a somewhat more than less
emancipated evening
had in return for consciousness
endowed him with a changeless grin

whereon a dozen staunch and leal
citizens did graze at pause
then fired by hypercivic zeal
sought newer pastures or because

swaddled with a frozen brook
of pinkest vomit out of eyes
which noticed nobody he looked
as if he did not care to rise

one hand did nothing on the vest
its wideflung friend clenched weakly dirt
while the mute trouserfly confessed
a button solemnly inert.

Brushing from whom the stiffened puke
i put him all into my arms
and staggered banged with terror through
a million billion trillion stars

(e. e. cummings)

Moments before his execution, a whiskey priest speaks to the young lieutenant who has hounded him down:
  "You say: 'God is love,'" the lieutenant said.

"Oh," the priest said, "that's another thing altogether— God *is* love. I don't say the heart doesn't feel a taste of it, but what a taste. The smallest glass of love mixed with a pint pot of ditch-water. We wouldn't recognize *that* love. It might even look like hate. It would be enough to scare us—God's love. It set fire to a bush in the desert, didn't it, and smashed open graves and set the dead walking in the dark? Oh, a man like me would run a mile to get away if he felt that love around."
                    (Graham Greene, *The Power and the Glory*)

Reading

Jesus finished washing his friends' feet, put on clothes again, and went back to his place at the table. "You understand what I've just done, don't you?" he asked. "You treat me as your teacher and your Lord. Fine; that's what we are to one another. And yet if I, your teacher and Lord, got down on my knees to you and washed your feet, then you should surely wash one another's feet. Let what I've just done to you be the gauge of your life. I've humbled myself before you. Now, go and do the same."
                                        (John 13:12–15)

Scriptural
Reading

Holy Friend,
as your Son enfleshed who you are,
so we, the Church, are your body now.
You have no hands on earth but mine.
It is through my eyes and my heart
that you now look with compassion on the world.
It is with my feet and my wits
that you have chosen to go about doing your will.
Your Son is the head of the person we have become.
Through my fusion into him,
I am fused into the aliveness of you,
and all I do today
is transfigured by your power.
Amen.

Closing

EVENING

Presence | Living God,
infuse me with your holiness.
Help me to heal.
Make me whole.
Keep me hale and hearty.
That's enough.

Grace: God of mercy and justice, let me know that in
your transforming hands, no gift of mine is small.

Psalm 131 | Bountiful God,
my life's too brief for wishful thinking,
hankering,
hungering for it all.
Whatever greatness I can offer
seems perhaps to those around me
pitiably small.
Still, I rest at ease in you,
enchanted as a child,
tranquil in its mother's arms,
willing even to be weaned.
It is your greatness I count on, my friend,
not my own.

i am a little church (no great cathedral)
far from the splendor and squalor of hurrying cities
—i do not worry if briefer days grow briefest,
i am not sorry when sun and rain make april

my life is the life of the reaper and the sower;
my prayers are prayers of earth's own clumsily striving
(finding and losing and laughing and crying) children
whose any sadness or joy is my grief or my gladness

around me surges a miracle of unceasing
birth and glory and death and resurrection:
over my sleeping self float flaming symbols
of hope, and i wake to a perfect patience of mountains

i am a little church (far from the frantic
world with its rapture and anguish) at peace with nature
—i do not worry if longer nights grow longest;
i am not sorry when silence becomes singing

winter by spring, i lift my diminutive spire to
merciful Him Whose only now is forever:
standing erect in the deathless truth of His presence
(welcoming humbly His light and proudly His darkness)

(e. e. cummings)

Hymn

Holy Friend,
your Son's first wish
at every meeting
was simply, "Peace."
For whatever ways I have unsettled that peace today,
I beg your forbearance.
For whatever peace I was able to create,
I am pleased.
Amen.

Closing

First Thursday

MORNING

Presence

Living God,
the numbers on my watch I think are time,
but they're not.
The real time for which you made me
are the moments out of time,
the times when you surprise me,
the times I say, "Oh, my God!"

Grace: Fire of Love, let me not be afraid to shine.

Psalm

Arise! Be radiant! Your light has come.
The glory of our God is alive in you,
no matter that the darkness seems to hem you round.
Let the blind grope toward your brightness;
let the weak warm themselves at your joy.
Open the eyes of your heart and see!
Can you feel them fumbling there in their dark?
Can you sense the dryness of their heart?
Ah! The light of God is in you,
the wellspring of Love in your soul.

(Isaiah 60:1–5)

i thank You God for most this amazing
day:for the leaping greenly spirits of trees
and a blue true dream of sky;and for everything
which is natural which is infinite which is yes

(i who have died am alive again today,
and this is the sun's birthday;this is the birth
day of life and of love and wings:and of the gay
great happening illimitably earth)

how should tasting touching hearing seeing
breathing any—lifted from the no
of all nothing—human merely being
doubt unimaginable You?

(now the ears of my ears awake and
now the eyes of my eyes are opened)

                                    (e. e. cummings)

Hymn

God, my friend,
I offer you this day.
Let all my prayer, work, joy, suffering today
join with the lives offered to you
by the whole People of God
and especially with our great Eucharist,
Jesus,
your Son and our Brother.
Let your Spirit be with me today,
especially in . . .
And I ask your loving concern today,
especially for my friend . . .
Remind me, through the day, that I am not alone.
Amen.

Offering

DAYTIME

Presence

Living God,
let me work with passion,
unafraid of burning out,
of being used,
of being called a fool.

Grace: God, let me be proud to have been chosen.

Psalm

The path lies straight before me,
and like a mother at the brink of birthing,
the fire you've conceived in me, Creator God,
is surging up toward life.
I writhe with the urge to begin,
to bring forth life,
to kindle hope,
to raise the dead into light.
Awake! Exult! He is born!
From the darkness of death comes the Light.
The dawn of the Christ is in my hands.

(Isaiah 26:16–19)

Hymn

Death closes all; but something ere the end,
Some work of noble note, may yet be done,
Not unbecoming men that strove with Gods.
The lights begin to twinkle from the rocks;
The long day wanes; the slow moon climbs; the deep
Moans round with many voices. Come, my friends,
'Tis not too late to seek a newer world.
Push off, and sitting well in order smite
The sounding furrows; for my purpose holds
To sail beyond the sunset, and the baths
Of all the western stars, until I die.
It may be that the gulfs will wash us down;
It may be we shall touch the Happy Isles,
And see the great Achilles, whom we knew.
Tho' much is taken, much abides; and tho'
We are not now that strength which in old days
Moved earth and heaven, that which we are, we are,—

One equal temper of heroic hearts,
Made weak by time and fate, but strong in will
To strive, to seek, to find, and not to yield.
                    (Alfred Lord Tennyson, "Ulysses")

Reading

In the beginning was *Power*, intelligent, loving, energiz-
ing. In the beginning was the *Word*, supremely capable of
mastering and moulding whatever might come into being
in the world of matter. In the beginning there were not
coldness and darkness: there was the *Fire*. This is the truth.
                    (Pierre Teilhard de Chardin, *Hymn of the Universe*)

Scriptural Reading

You are the salt of the earth! But if salt loses its tang, what
can put zest back into it? It is lifeless as the red clay dust of
the road.

    You are the light of the world! You're supposed to stick
out like a sore thumb! If there's only one light in the room,
do you hide it under a trash can? Of course not! You put it
up there where it can shine on everybody in the house. Just
so. Your light must *shine*, so everyone around can *see* it!
Not you, your light—the light which is the presence of the
Holy Spirit in you. Then what excuse can they have not to
praise him?
                    (Matthew 5:13–16)

Closing

God of all goodness,
distract me from my fear,
my shyness,
my slavery to what *they* will think.
If only I can keep my eyes off myself
and on you,
if only I can rid myself of my gravity,
I can walk on water,
on air,
on fire.
Amen.

EVENING

Presence | Living God,
you've been with me today
even when I was unaware.
Now, as the day ends,
let me be aware.

Grace: Holy Friend, I am unworthy that you come into my home, but only say the word and I am worthy.

Psalm 91 | I live in the shelter of my creator,
my refuge, my fortress,
my God in whom I trust.
I am wrapped in the web of God's wings,
with angels at my side
to guard me in all God's ways.
They will carry me in the palms of their hands,
lest I dash my foot against a stone.
You, my God, proclaim,
"Cling to me,
call on me,
entrust your safety and honor to me.
I protect all who know my name."

Hymn | It is a beauteous evening, calm and free,
The holy time is quiet as a Nun
Breathless with adoration; the broad sun
Is sinking down in its tranquillity;
The gentleness of heaven broods o'er the Sea:
Listen! the mighty Being is awake,
And doth with his eternal motion make
A sound like thunder—everlastingly.
Dear Child! dear Girl! that walkest with me here,
If thou appear untouched by solemn thought,
Thy nature is not therefore less divine:
Thou liest in Abraham's bosom all the year;
And worshipp'st at the Temple's inner shrine,
God being with thee when we know it not.

(William Wordsworth, Sonnet 30)

Holy Friend,
I've finished another page
and close the book again.
The rest of the story that the two of us write
can wait.
Amen.

Closing

First Friday

MORNING

Presence | Living God,
the day begins at sixes and sevens,
bits and pieces,
one-thing-after-another.
Before we begin, help me see
that I won't remake the world today,
just shake a few more pieces into place,
if I can.

Grace: Let me be still and know that you are God.

Psalm 65 | Merciful God,
at times my faults fragment me,
when weakness cracks resolve,
and my soul sifts through my fingers and away.
Yet, I come to you and boldly beg you:
energize my will;
retrieve the scattered pieces of my soul.
And, as it was in the beginning,
you speak your Word,
and chaos hushes to a stillness,
and the clamor of the waves becomes becalmed,
and the land thrusts up and surges into life:
rivers tumble from the hills,
valleys clothe themselves in wheat,
and tumult is transfigured into power.
You're not content with order.
For you, there must be life!
What shouts of joy!
What singing!

It is not growing like a tree
 In bulk, doth make man better be;
Or standing long an oak, three hundred year,
To fall a log at last, dry, bald, and sear;
  A lily of a day
   Is fairer far, in May,
 Although it fall and die that night,
  It was a plant and flower of Light.
In small proportions we just beauties see;
And in short measures life may perfect be.
                    (Ben Jonson, "The Noble Nature")

Hymn

God, my friend,
I offer you this day.
Let all my prayer, work, joy, suffering today
join with the lives offered to you
by the whole People of God
and especially with our great Eucharist,
Jesus,
your Son and our Brother.
Let your Spirit be with me today,
especially in . . .
And I ask your loving concern today,
especially for my friend . . .
Remind me, through the day, that I am not alone.
Amen.

Offering

DAYTIME

Presence | Living God,
only when I am empty can you fill me;
only when I am poor can you enrich me;
only when I serve can you enoble me.

Grace: In order to learn triumph, teach me to surrender,
Faithful Friend.

Psalm | My soul proclaims the presence of God,
and my spirit exults in God,
my ransom from lowliness.
This day and all days I am blessed,
because you, Almighty, have worked miracles in me.
Holy is your name.
Your forbearance is unending,
for those who trust in you.
You pluck the preening from their perches;
you tumble tyrants from their thrones.
But you lift the lowly to their feet
and fill all emptiness,
while the sated are sent
empty
away.

(Luke 1:46–53)

Hymn | Nature's first green is gold,
Her hardest hue to hold.
Her early leaf's a flower;
But only so an hour.
Then leaf subsides to leaf.
So Eden sank to grief,
So dawn goes down to day.
Nothing gold can stay.

(Robert Frost, "Nothing Gold Can Stay")

"It is not that I am avaricious. The Pyx I keep for the sake of the House"—almost she was able to think, "for the sake of God,"—but let that pass; she'd be honest and set her claim too low rather than too high. "And the gold," she thought, "it is not that I love the gold itself." She bent lower over the strings of her lute. Gold was a soft cushion to sit on. Gold was a rod to rule with. Gold bought things of good craftsmanship, things that were beautiful, things that made the heart rejoice. Without gold man in this world went very nakedly and wretchedly; with gold, strong and hearty, he might the better praise God. "Gold," she thought, "it's gold that bought this fair lute," and suddenly struck a full chord in which the voice of the strings mingled tingling sweetness and a sombre compassionate solemnity. She listened while the notes pulsated, dwindled and died.

Without raising her head she looked up at the old woman who sat mumbling with her lips like a rabbit.

"Surely," said the Prioress, in a low but defiant tone, "surely gold is good."

(H. F. M. Prescott, *The Man on a Donkey*)

Reading

Why do you fuss so about your food and your body and your clothes? Surely life means more than that. Look up! See the sparrows flirting in the air? They don't sow or reap or store up for tomorrow? And yet your creator repays their forage with food for the day. Surely, you're worth more than they. For all your fussing, can you add an instant to your life?

And clothes. More fuss. Look out at the lilies in the field. They neither toil nor spin, but in all that dryness, their roots grip down, and even the silks of Solomon are not like their silken skins. If God takes such care to array weeds, which are here today and gone tomorrow, will God forget you—when you will last forever, even though you think you have to do it all yourself?

(Matthew 6:25–34)

Scriptural Reading

Merciful God,
make me wise enough to let you do that:
be my guide and protector.
Amen.

Closing

EVENING

Presence

Living God,
my greatest enemy
is envy.
When everyone around me calls me fool,
remind me that your emblem
is a corpse upon a cross.

Grace: God, let me cling to what is real.

Psalm 73

Patient God, you caught me again
on the point of stumbling,
envying the arrogant,
watching the wicked and their wealth.
No pain for them!
Their bodies pulse and gleam;
their condescension oozes out like fat;
they are sly, slick, slipshod.
And they seem to make sense:
"How will God know?"
"Has God nothing better to do than spy?"
"Come on! Are you some kind of saint?"
And there I was, the fool—
simple, well-intentioned clod.
"Face it. I've just one life to live.
After, God will forgive, no matter what."
But you had me by the hand,
and I paused,
and I watched,
and they fell
like phantoms in a morning dream.

Thou art indeed just, Lord, if I contend
With thee; but, sir, so what I plead is just.
Why do sinners' ways prosper? and why must
Disappointment all I endeavour end?
    Wert thou my enemy, O thou my friend,
How wouldst thou worse, I wonder, than thou dost
Defeat, thwart me? Oh, the sots and thralls of lust
Do in spare hours more thrive than I that spend,
Sir, life upon thy cause. See, banks and brakes
Now, leaved how thick! laced they are again
With fretty chervil, look, and fresh wind shakes
Them; birds build—but not I build; no, but strain,
Time's eunuch, and not breed one work that wakes.
Mine, O thou lord of life, send my roots rain.
                            (Gerard Manley Hopkins)

Holy Friend,
the most wasted parts of my day
have been when I said, "If only . . ."
But doing what you ask is lonely.
And this moment is lonely.
You've been there.
You know.
Amen.

First Saturday

MORNING

Presence

Living God,
you are the Timeless, in my soul.
Remind me when I take a stand,
I do not stand alone.

Grace: Timeless Friend, let me know you, the one Truth.

Psalm

Child, don't be shackled by shame;
let guilt turn you back toward the truth.
Don't contend against truth,
for truth is the will of the Lord.
Don't make claims with your mouth
that you don't carry out with your hands.
Don't be a lion alone
but mute in the face of a crowd.
Don't be cowed by the great;
speak out, or forswear your soul.

(Ecclesiasticus 4:20–28)

Hymn

I cannot ope mine eyes,
But thou art ready there to catch
My morning-soul and sacrifice:
Then we must needs for that day make a match.

My God, what is a heart?
Silver, or gold, or precious stone,
Or starre, or rainbow, or a part
Of all these things, or all of them in one?

My God, what is a heart,
That thou shouldst it so eye, and wooe,
Pouring upon it all thy art,
As if that thou hadst nothing els to do?

Indeed, mans whole estate
Amounts (and richly) to serve thee:
He did not heav'n and earth create,
Yet studies them, not him by whom they be.

Teach me thy love to know;
That this new light, which now I see,
May both the work and workman show:
Then by a sunne-beam I will climbe to thee.

(George Herbert, "Mattens")

Offering

God, my friend,
I offer you this day.
Let all my prayer, work, joy, suffering today
join with the lives offered to you
by the whole People of God
and especially with our great Eucharist,
Jesus,
your Son and our Brother.
Let your Spirit be with me today,
especially in . . .
And I ask your loving concern today,
especially for my friend . . .
Remind me, through the day, that I am not alone.
Amen.

DAYTIME

Presence

Living God,
if you should ask some awful gift of me,
let me realize how wonderful
that you trust me enough
to ask it.

> **Grace:** O God, to know who I am, I must first know who
> you are.

Psalm

From the heart of the maelstrom, God answered Job:
"Who is this—another god?—
reworking my will with witless words?
Ah, then. Brace yourself, battler!
It is my turn to ask, yours to answer.
Where were you when I laid the foundations of the earth?
When the plans were drawn, was I forced to submit them?
Were you there when I set the cornerstone of it,
when the fire-folk blazed in the skies
and all the stars of morning shouted for joy?
Do you remember the birth of the sea,
when it tumbled in tumult from its womb,
and I swaddled it in mist and cloud?
You, who would counsel me,
speak!"

(Job 38:1–11)

Hymn

Mine eyes have seen the glory of the coming of the Lord;
He is trampling out the vintage where the grapes of wrath
        are stored;
He hath loosed the fateful lightning of His terrible, swift
        sword;
    His truth is marching on. . . .

He has sounded forth the trumpet that shall never call
        retreat;
He is sifting out the hearts of men before His judgment-
        seat:
O, be swift, my soul, to answer Him! be jubilant, my feet!
    Our God is marching on.

In the beauty of the lilies Christ was born across the sea,
With a glory in His bosom that transfigures you and me;
As He died to make men holy, let us live to make men free,
   While God is marching on.
                        (Adapted from Julia Ward Howe,
                        "Battle-Hymn of the Republic")

Reading

Already the new men are dotted here and there all over the earth. Some, as I have admitted, are still hardly recognisable: but others can be recognised. Every now and then one meets them. Their very voices and faces are different from ours; stronger, quieter, happier, more radiant. They begin where most of us leave off. . . . They will not be very like the idea of "religious people" which you have formed from your general reading. They do not draw attention to themselves. You tend to think that you are being kind to them when they are really being kind to you. They love you more than other men do, but they need you less.
                        (C. S. Lewis, *Mere Christianity*)

Scriptural Reading

Do not fool yourselves that I've come to bring peace. Oh, no. Not peace, but a sword that sunders. There will be times when you must choose between my will and your father's, or your mother's, or your inlaws'. Because of me, you will face enemies in your own household.

   But anyone who chooses his father's or his mother's will over mine is not worthy to walk with me. And walk you will, and always toward the cross. Pick up your cross then, today, and come—or you are not worthy of me. If you hold back your self, your life will be lost. If you surrender your self, you will find life.

                        (Matthew 10:34–39)

Closing

God of power,
those who have easy lives
have no story worth telling.
I have only one life,
and that all too brief.
Despite my fear,
my frailty,
my faltering,
make my one life a thing worth dying for.
Amen.

EVENING

Presence | Living God,
come aside and rest awhile with me.
Help me to stop groping, griping, gaping around.
Help me to see.

> **Grace:** Ever-present God, allow me to forgive myself for
> not being you.

Psalm 32 | How gifted I am with forgiveness
when my God forgets I have sinned,
like a child, without grudges or guile.
But without me, God's healing is helpless.
Before, I was stiff-necked and stubborn,
my soul grappled grimly in spite,
as gnarled as the pit of a peach.
But finally I came to my senses
and let myself drop to my knees,
where insolence knows
that the bridle and bit aren't to break me,
but to bring me where God bids me go.

Hymn | Wilt thou forgive that sinne where I begunne,
    Which is my sin, though it were done before?
Wilt thou forgive those sinnes, through which I runne,
    And do run still: though still I do deplore?
        When thou hast done, thou hast not done,
           For, I have more.

Wilt thou forgive that sinne by which I'have wonne
    Others to sinne? and, made my sinne their doore?
Wilt thou forgive that sinne which I did shunne
    A yeare, or two: but wallowed in, a score?
        When thou hast done, thou hast not done,
           For I have more.

I have a sinne of feare, that when I have spunne
    My last thred, I shall perish on the shore;
Sweare by thy selfe, that at my death thy sonne
    Shall shine as he shines now, and heretofore;
        And, having done that, Thou haste done,
           I feare no more.
        (John Donne, "A Hymne to God the Father")

Holy Friend,
as you have graciously forgiven
my shyness,
my shortcuts,
my shirking,
give me the good grace to forgive
my self.
Amen.

Closing

❧ Second Week ❧

Second Sunday

Presence

Living God,
you open up another day
with all the ease of a baker,
unshuttering the sun,
setting our daily bread to rise.
I'm not that easy to unclose or rouse.
But give me time.

Grace: God, let me know that you remember my name.

Psalm

O God, you are the fire in all that lives.
Up in black night, sparks of you shimmer and ignite,
and at dawn you shoulder the horizon, blazing.
You roil the deep and thunder in the air.
It is you, Yahweh, ruler of all, who speaks:
"When the great carouse of the heavens ceases,
when the steady stream of birth-rebirth stands still—
Listen!—
only then is there a chance you've slipped my mind.
When you've measured the arid cold from star to star,
when you've tallied the flecks of sand beneath the seas,
Come back then and ask if I remember.
I can no more forget you, love, than you can."
(Jeremiah 31:35–37)

When God at first made man,
Having a glasse of blessings standing by;
Let us (said he) poure on him all we can:
Let the worlds riches, which dispersed lie,
        Contract into a span.

        So strength first made a way;
Then beautie flow'd, then wisdome, honour, pleasure:
When almost all was out, God made a stay,
Perceiving that alone of all his treasure
        Rest in the bottome lay.

        For if I should (said he)
Bestow this jewell also on my creature,
He would adore my gifts in stead of me,
And rest in Nature, not the God of Nature:
        So both should losers be.

        Yet let him keep the rest,
But keep them with repining restlesnesse:
Let him be rich and wearie, that at least,
If goodnesse leade him not, yet wearinesse
        May tosse him to my breast.
                    (George Herbert, "The Pulley")

Hymn

God, my friend,
I offer you this day.
Let all my prayer, work, joy, suffering today
join with the lives offered to you
by the whole People of God
and especially with our great Eucharist,
Jesus,
your Son and our Brother.
Let your Spirit be with me today,
especially in . . .
And I ask your loving concern today,
especially for my friend . . .
Remind me, through the day, that I am not alone.
Amen.

Offering

DAYTIME

Presence | Living God,
I grow dizzy in this whirligig world,
shunted from hither to yon and back.
Come off with me awhile,
and tell me where we're going.

Grace: Holy Wisdom, show me the way, so that I can lead.

Psalm 94 | God, my God,
I blunder around the day
like someone blind through a minefield.
Voices volley at me from everywhere:
—"Come this way!"
—"Here, fool!"
—"No, here!"
I grope about for you, grasping only air,
scrabbling through scrub,
whimpering.
Can you who conjured sound not hear my voice?
Can you who dreamed the light not see I'm lost?

"Stand still! Still.
Don't rage around,
rummaging the dark for me.
Let me
find you."
And you took hold of me,
there in that still place,
the silent center of the storm.

Hymn | The leaves are falling, falling as from way off,
as though far gardens withered in the skies;
they are falling with denying gestures.

And in the nights the heavy earth is falling
from all the stars down into loneliness.

We all are falling. This hand falls.
And look at others: it is in them all.

And yet there is one who holds this falling
endlessly gently in his hands.

(Rainer Maria Rilke, "Autumn")

A climber was pawing up the last rocky face toward the mountaintop. Only a few more feet. But suddenly a rock slipped out from underfoot, and down he careered in a shower of gravel and rocks toward the granite lip—beyond which was nothing but empty air.

Just at the last instant he snagged the root of a bush and clung there, hanging over the edge. Panting, shellacked with sweat, he threw back his head and howled, "Help me! Is anybody up there? Help!"

And a great voice came from nowhere: "Yes! I'll help you. I'm God. Just let go. I'll catch you."

The climber exhausted a deep breath and stared down through his dangling toes to the floor of the valley, almost invisible below. He took another breath and cried, "Is there anybody *else* up there?"

(Author unknown)

Reading

It was now about noon. The sun hid itself, and darkness covered the whole earth. At three, there was a great shudder, as if the curtain of the Temple had shredded and God had deserted the holy of holies. Then Jesus cried out in a loud voice: "Father! Into your hands I commend my spirit!" And with those final words, he yielded up his soul.

(Luke 23:44–46)

Scriptural Reading

God of mercy,
the sin of Adam and Eve
was to try to go it alone,
to take history out of your hands,
to be free of you.
Remind me that I needn't go it alone
because I am not.
Amen.

Closing

EVENING

Presence | Living God,
the day slides away westward,
the rhythms settle slowly down.
Let that way of gentling things,
gentle me.

Grace: God, you have a peace that I find no other place.

Psalm 104 | Creator of the universe,
the year is a fusion of law and surprise,
birthing and death,
and then on.
Winter cracks and dribbles into streams;
life seeps up and shimmers into bloom,
swells into the heaviness of fruit,
shrivels, freezes, fragments to seed again.
The year is a spiral of soaring life:
the fly in the frog gives life to the frog,
and becomes a flycatcher itself;
the frog becomes part of the long-legged crane,
and the frog can leap into the skies;
I am fed by the flesh of those sun-winged birds,
and their flying is turned into hope,
and I place my life in your transforming hands,
and I become deathless in you.

All day thy wings have fanned,
At that far height, the cold thin atmosphere,
Yet stoop not, weary, to the welcome land
    Though the dark night is near

    And soon that toil shall end;
Soon shalt thou find a summer home, and rest,
And scream among thy fellows; reeds shall bend,
    Soon, o'er thy sheltered nest.

    Thou'rt gone, the abyss of heaven
Hath swallowed up thy form; yet, on my heart
Deeply hath sunk the lesson thou hast given,
    And shall not soon depart.

    He who, from zone to zone,
Guides through the boundless sky thy certain flight,
In the long way that I must tread alone
    Will lead my steps aright.
                    (William Cullen Bryant, "To a Waterfowl")

Closing

Holy Friend,
you need no rest;
I do.
So—please take this only half in jest—
I now leave the night
to burglars,
bats,
and you.
Amen.

Second Monday

MORNING

Presence | Living God,
if I were to fail this morning meeting of the day,
I know I could "get through" anyway.
But I ask for more than mere survival.
For that hope, I can blame only you.

Grace: God, give me a sign. I don't care how small.

Psalm 121 | God-Guardian,
I raise my eyes to the mountains,
shadowed against the sun,
and I hear your voice in the distance:
"Come, pilgrim. Climb to me."
I've no great urge to be roaming;
too much to be done at home.
But you call—incessant, insistent.
So, grumbling, I rise and go.
The sun's a blaze on my shoulders;
paths slip out from under my feet.
But a cloud like a hand seems to shadow me;
failing, I do not fall.
You've been with my journey leaving;
be with me coming home.

Hymn | When I consider how my light is spent,
    Ere half my days, in this dark world and wide,
    And that one talent which is death to hide,
    Lodged with me useless, though my soul more bent
To serve therewith my maker, and present
    My true account, lest he returning chide,
    Doth God exact day-labour, light denied,
    I fondly ask; but Patience, to prevent

That murmur, soon replies, God doth not need
    Either man's work or his own gifts, who best
    Bear his mild yoke, they serve him best, his state
Is kingly. Thousands at his bidding speed,
    And post o'er land and ocean without rest:
    They also serve who only stand and wait.
                    (John Milton, Sonnet 26)

Offering

God, my friend,
I offer you this day.
Let all my prayer, work, joy, suffering today
join with the lives offered to you
by the whole People of God
and especially with our great Eucharist,
Jesus,
your Son and our Brother.
Let your Spirit be with me today,
especially in . . .
And I ask your loving concern today,
especially for my friend . . .
Remind me, through the day, that I am not alone.
Amen.

🌺

DAYTIME

Presence

Living God,
like Cinderella,
I'm unaware of the magic in ordinary things:
the work,
the people I share it with,
and, not least, myself.
Help me understand
that the commonplace
is what you've given me
to alchemize.

Grace: God, let me find you, wherever.

Psalm 31 | There's more challenging parts in this play, to be sure.
Not the lead, God, of course. That's yours.
The arch-villain's part is a role I've tried,
but it calls for a . . . stature I lack.
I'm not right for the unsullied maid or the knight,
the fool or the witch or the ghoul.
They're all more . . . extreme than the talent I have,
and I don't long for the lead anymore.
I don't mind that I'm assigned to the menial roles:
serve the meal, open doors, point the way.
I am pleased to announce the entrance of the Host,
and fade back to the chorus and sing.
But the roles that I play seem created from glass:
they look *through* me, as if I weren't there.
And the Lead said, "That's fine, friend.
It's just what I want.
You're not here for applause.
Just play."

Hymn | Love bade me welcome: yet my soul drew back,
                    Guiltie of dust and sinne.
But quick-ey'd Love, observing me grow slack
                    From my first entrance in,
Drew nearer to me, sweetly questioning,
                    If I lack'd any thing.

A guest, I answer'd, worthy to be here:
                    Love said, You shall be he.
I the unkinde, ungratefull? Ah my deare,
                    I cannot look on thee.
Love took my hand, and smiling did reply,
                    Who made the eyes but I?

Truth Lord, but I have marr'd them: let my shame
                    Go where it doth deserve.
And know you not, sayes Love, who bore the blame?
                    My deare, then I will serve.
You must sit down, sayes Love, and taste my meat:
                    So I did sit and eat.
                              (George Herbert, "Love")

They are the only ones capable of understanding joy. Everybody else is too weak for joy. Joy would kill anybody but these meek. They are the clean of heart. They see God. He does their will, because His will is their own. He does all that they want, because He is the One Who desires all their desires. They are the only ones who have everything that they can desire. Their freedom is without limit. They reach out for us to comprehend our misery and drown it in the tremendous expansion of their own innocence, that washes the world with its light.

(Thomas Merton, *New Seeds of Contemplation*)

Reading

Misfortune is often a doorway, and good luck a dead end.

Some windfalls you end up paying for yourself, but some intimidating, infuriating encroachments on your time enrich you a hundredfold.

Honors laid on from outside soon grow thin and forgotten; honor forged from within may be unseen, but it can never be taken away, only surrendered.

Even inferior fools can delight the mob for a moment; the wise who listen with vulnerable hearts are beyond death.

Gratitude is rare, but longing for it is obsessive; forswearing gratitude is the final test of love.

(Ecclesiasticus 20:9–17)

Scriptural Reading

Patient Friend,
I'd like to say I believe all that.
But something still unredeemed in me balks.
Jesus felt it, too—
when only one leper came back,
when none of them ever really understood,
when they thought his availability was limitless.
But he went on.
Amen.

Closing

EVENING

Presence

Living God,
there were times today
I wanted to say, "Just leave me *alone!*"
I realize now
I never really meant that.

Grace: God, grant me the wisdom that leads to peace.

Psalm

See him, my Son, my chosen.
My soul delights in him!
I have infused my Spirit into him,
that he might lead all peoples to me.
He does not cry out or shout
or bellow about the streets.
He will not reject the bruised or weak,
the irresolute or fainthearted,
if only they will try.
Faithful, he comes bearing justice,
and the outlands yearn for his coming.

(Isaiah 42:1–4)

Hymn

When fishes flew and forests walked
    And figs grew upon thorn,
Some moment when the moon was blood
    Then surely I was born.

With monstrous head and sickening cry
    And ears like errant wings,
The devil's walking parody
    On all four-footed things.

The tattered outlaw of the earth,
    Of ancient crooked will;
Starve, scourge, deride me: I am dumb,
    I keep my secret still.

Fools! For I also had my hour;
    One far fierce hour and sweet:
There was a shout about my ears,
    And palms before my feet.

(Gilbert K. Chesterton, "The Donkey")

Holy Friend,
had I done something heinous today,
my thought would be focused on me.
Since most of my fumblings were quite unoriginal,
I'm free to focus on you.
Amen.

Closing

Second Tuesday

MORNING

Presence

Living God,
if I'm to have anything to tell today,
let me pause and listen.

Grace: In patience, Holy Friend, I will possess my soul.

Psalm

A sower went out scattering seed
in great angel-wing fans, side to side.
Some filtered down on the pathway to town,
and passersby trampled it in the dust;
what was left was pecked up by the birds.
Some landed in cracks in the rock and caught
but, waterless, withered and died.
Some seed took root among clutches of thorn
and grew up through the barbs and was choked.
But some grain fell into soil he'd prepared,
and it gripped and grew and yielded him bread.
Let those who can hear take heed.

(Luke 8:5–8)

A noiseless patient spider,
I mark'd where on a little promontory it stood isolated,
Mark'd how to explore the vacant vast surrounding,
It launch'd forth filament, filament, filament, out of itself.
Ever unreeling them, ever tirelessly speeding them.

And you O my soul where you stand,
Surrounded, detached, in measureless oceans of space,
Ceaselessly musing, venturing, throwing, seeking the
       spheres to connect them,
Till the bridge you will need be form'd, till the ductile
       anchor hold,
Till the gossamer thread you fling catch somewhere, O my
       soul.
           (Walt Whitman, "A Noiseless Patient Spider")

God, my friend,
I offer you this day.
Let all my prayer, work, joy, suffering today
join with the lives offered to you
by the whole People of God
and especially with our great Eucharist,
Jesus,
your Son and our Brother.
Let your Spirit be with me today,
especially in . . .
And I ask your loving concern today,
especially for my friend . . .
Remind me, through the day, that I am not alone.
Amen.

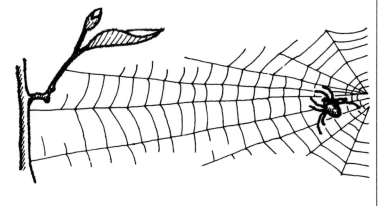

DAYTIME

Presence | Living God,
some say the most immobilizing sin
is the feverish paralysis of lust,
focusing all the yearnings of heart and soul
into the loins.
But it's not.
It is the solitary arrogance of despair,
condensing all the yearnings of the universe
into oneself,
alone.
I am tempted by both, my redeemer.
Tarry not too long.

Grace: God, let me lose myself, to be found.

Psalm | God of hope,
I thought that I had known who you are. But no.
I had heard of you, as others might describe a friend.
It was only in that empty wasteland that we met,
and wrestled among the rocks, till I relented.
Overpowered by who you are and who I am, I bowed,
and you adopted me there, to guard as the core of your eye.
Then, like an eagle, hovering, spreading great wings,
you lofted me, confident, into the air with you.

(Deuteronomy 32:10–11)

Hymn | We thinke that *Paradise* and *Calvarie*,
    Christs Crosse, and *Adams* tree, stood in one place;
Looke Lord, and finde both *Adams* met in me;
    As the first *Adams* sweat surrounds my face,
    May the last *Adams* blood my soule embrace.

So, in his purple wrapp'd receive mee Lord,
    By these his thornes give me his other Crowne;
And as to others soules I preach'd thy word,
    Be this my Text, my Sermon to mine owne,
    Therefore that he may raise the Lord throws down.
(John Donne, "Hymne to God My God, In My Sicknesse")

You cannot play with the animal in you without becoming wholly animal, play with falsehood without forfeiting your right to truth, play with cruelty without losing your sensitivity of mind. He who wants to keep his garden tidy doesn't reserve a plot for weeds.

(Dag Hammarskjöld, *Markings*)

Reading

Job answered God: "I know now you are the power from which all power takes its name. What you conceive, comes to be. I have smeared your designs with my muddy-witted words, monologuing on matters beyond the understanding of my mind. Then, I knew you only by hearsay. But—now—I see you with my eyes. I repent my pretentiousness, and I bow before you."

(Job 42:1–6)

Scriptural Reading

God of peace,
help me to find peace
somewhere between my vaulting ambitions
and my timid expectations.
Amen.

Closing

EVENING

Presence | Living God,
as you transform bread and wine into your Son,
transform the bits and pieces of my day
into a gift I can offer without excuse.

Grace: Creator God, so near to grandeur is our dust.

Psalm | The people who had walked in darkness
have seen a great light!
Out of the gloom, it dawns.
You have awakened in us a quake of joy!
The yoke is transformed to a regal collar,
the overseer's lash to a scepter.
For unto us a child is born, a son is given,
and the governance shall be upon his shoulder.
And his names shall be trumpeted!
Wonderful! Counselor! The Mighty God!
The Everlasting Father!
The Prince of Peace!

(Isaiah 9:1–5)

Hymn | Earth gets its price for what Earth gives us;
    The beggar is taxed for a corner to die in,
The priest hath his fee who comes and shrives us,
    We bargain for the graves we lie in;
At the devil's booth are all things sold,
Each ounce of dross costs its ounce of gold;
    For a cap and bells our lives we pay,
Bubbles we buy with a whole soul's tasking:
    'T is heaven alone that is given away,
'T is only God may be had for the asking.

(James Russell Lowell, "The Vision of Sir Launfal")

Holy Friend,
the poet says
you alone can be had without price.
That's not precisely true.
But I will pay.
Amen.

Closing

Second Wednesday

MORNING

Presence | Living God,
fuel my heart with trust,
~~my will with nerve,~~
my mind with you.
And I am ready.

Grace: Holy God, my will is to do the will of you who send me.

Psalm 103 | My soul blesses you, my God, and your holy name!
Forgiving, healing, redeeming, crowning—us!
You are always at the side of the downtrodden.
Tender, slow to anger, loving, you annul our sins,
flinging them as far as the east is from the west.
What can I give for all you have done to me?
"Go you, and do the same: forgive, heal, redeem, crown.
And you will find life."

Hymn | Let not young souls be smothered out before
They do quaint deeds and fully flaunt their pride.
It is the world's one crime its babes grow dull,
Its poor are ox-like, limp and leaden-eyed.

Not that they starve, but starve so dreamlessly,
Not that they sow, but that they seldom reap,
Not that they serve, but have no gods to serve,
Not that they die but that they die like sheep.
(Vachel Lindsay, "The Leaden-eyed")

God, my friend,
I offer you this day.
Let all my prayer, work, joy, suffering today
join with the lives offered to you
by the whole People of God
and especially with our great Eucharist,
Jesus,
your Son and our Brother.
Let your Spirit be with me today,
especially in . . .
And I ask your loving concern today,
especially for my friend . . .
Remind me, through the day, that I am not alone.
Amen.

Offering

DAYTIME

Presence

Living God,
My downfall is asking: "But what's in this for me?"
Remind me of the simple answer:
everything—
you.

Grace: Gracious God, let me set myself aside.

Psalm 30

When I prosper, I am the commander of my soul;
I make merry, and nothing can shake me.
But then, my God, you hide your face from me.
I cry, and there is nothing but the silence,
and I am "here as on a darkling plain
where ignorant armies clash by night."
Gracious God, have pity on my loneliness.
How useful are my hands without your hand?
Turn my mourning into dancing,
turn my self-pity into joy,
that I may praise you.

Hymn

GOD moves in a mysterious way,
   His wonders to perform;
He plants his footsteps in the sea,
   And rides upon the storm. . . .

Judge not the LORD by feeble sense,
   But trust him for his grace;
Behind a frowning providence,
   He hides a smiling face.

His purposes will ripen fast,
   Unfolding ev'ry hour;
The bud may have a bitter taste,
   But sweet will be the flow'r.

Blind unbelief is sure to err,
   And scan his work in vain;
GOD is his own interpreter,
      And he will make it plain.
         (William Cowper, "Light Shining Out of Darkness")

The most beautiful and deepest experience a man can have is the sense of the mysterious. It is the underlying principle of religion as well as of all serious endeavour in art and in science. . . . He who never had this experience seems to me, if not dead, then at least blind. The sense that behind anything that can be experienced there is a something that our mind cannot grasp and whose beauty and sublimity reaches us only indirectly and as feeble reflexion, *this* is *religiousness*. In *this* sense I am religious. To me it suffices to wonder at these secrets and to attempt humbly to grasp with my mind a mere image of the lofty structure of all that there is.

(Albert Einstein, "My Credo") | **Reading**

We have a wisdom to offer, to those wise enough to sense its truth. It is not the mirror-mad philosophy of our age, that "humans are the measure of all things," nor that of our leaders who preach dominance and lead us toward destruction. What we speak is the mysterious wisdom of God: the scandal of the cross from which hung the world's salvation, the glorious Son of God. Had our rulers honestly sought the Truth, they would not have hanged him. It is written: "Eye has not seen, ear has not heard, nor has it ever dawned within a human mind what has been made ready for those who love God."

(1 Corinthians 2:6–9) | **Scriptural Reading**

Gracious God,
when I am certain
that I now understand you, this world, my meaning,
remind me I am not.
Amen. | **Closing**

EVENING

Presence | Living God,
as the day and I wind down,
let me pause and see
what is true
beneath what I thought was true.

Grace: Light, open the eyes of my eyes.

**Psalm 37
and
Philippians
4:8–9** | I lay small claim on what the world holds dear,
and yet I have treasure no moth can ravage,
no rust corrode.
You, God, have invaded this world; your Reign is come,
in which rich people's plenty is powerless,
so much devalued paper.
The treasury of God honors only
all that is true,
all that is noble,
all that is honest, pure, admirable,
decent, virtuous, worthy of praise—
whatever cannot be measured
by the scales, clocks, counters of the rich.
As it was in the beginning,
the essential is invisible.

Whose woods these are I think I know.
His house is in the village though;
He will not see me stopping here
To watch his woods fill up with snow.

My little horse must think it queer
To stop without a farmhouse near
Between the woods and frozen lake
This darkest evening of the year.

He gives his harness bells a shake
To ask if there is some mistake.
The only other sound's the sweep
Of easy wind and downy flake.

The woods are lovely, dark and deep,
But I have promises to keep,
And miles to go before I sleep,
And miles to go before I sleep.
  (Robert Frost, "Stopping by Woods on a Snowy Evening")

Holy Friend,
I am not here to check my celestial solvency.
I will leave that—and my soul—
to you.
Amen.

Second Thursday

MORNING

Presence Living God,
I pause here before setting out
to be sure the seed I sow,
the person I am,
is yours.

Grace: God, if you are to fulfill me, I must let go.

Psalm The hour has come for my death to bring glory.
I tell you, and there is no avoiding it,
unless the grain of wheat falls into the ground—and dies,
it remains what it seems: just a grain of wheat.
But if it dies—ah!—the harvest!
Whoever dote on themselves destroy themselves,
preserving what they seem to the world to be.
But those who sacrifice what they seem
are already living eternal life.
Whoever follows me must minister with me,
forgetting self,
and it is the eternal, loving God who will remember.
(John 12:23–26)

One of the Magi muses:

All this was a long time ago, I remember,
And I would do it again, but set down
This set down
This: were we led all that way for
Birth or Death? There was a Birth, certainly,
We had evidence and no doubt. I had seen birth and
        death,
But had thought they were different; this Birth was
Hard and bitter agony for us, like Death, our death.
We returned to our places, these Kingdoms,
But no longer at ease here, in the old dispensation,
With an alien people clutching their gods.
I should be glad of another death.
                    (T. S. Eliot, "Journey of the Magi")

Hymn

God, my friend,
I offer you this day.
Let all my prayer, work, joy, suffering today
join with the lives offered to you
by the whole People of God
and especially with our great Eucharist,
Jesus,
your Son and our Brother.
Let your Spirit be with me today,
especially in . . .
And I ask your loving concern today,
especially for my friend . . .
Remind me, through the day, that I am not alone.
Amen.

Offering

DAYTIME

Presence | Living God,
you have not allowed me the illusion
of "Live and let live."
As you ransomed me,
at times against my will,
I must ransom the unwilling too.

Grace: Holy Friend, let me be unafraid to invite them
home.

Psalm | As water smothers fire, kindness quenches sin.
Refuse not the poor a livelihood nor tantalize the needy.
Fuel not the grievances of those already fiery-tempered.
Distract yourself not from the sick and silent-suffering.
Make no woman or man beg for dignity.
As God is, be parent to the orphaned and family to the
bereft.
There is only one law: you must be kind.
If you seek mercy, you will find it in yourself—
or nowhere.

(Ecclesiasticus 4:1–10)

Hymn | What if this present were the worlds last night?
Marke in my heart, O Soule, where thou dost dwell,
The picture of Christ crucified, and tell
Whether that countenance can thee affright,
Teares in his eyes quench the amazing light,
Blood fills his frownes, which from his pierc'd head fell.
And can that tongue adjudge thee unto hell,
Which pray'd forgivenesse for his foes fierce spight?

(John Donne, Holy Sonnet 13)

I should like you to prove that you love God and me, his
servant and yours, in the following way. There should be
no friar in the whole world who has fallen into sin, no
matter how far he has fallen, who will ever fail to find your
forgiveness for the asking, if he will only look into your
eyes. And if he does not ask forgiveness, you should ask
him if he wants it. And should he appear before you again
a thousand times, you should love him more than you love
me, so that you may draw him to God.

(Saint Francis of Assisi)

Reading

If you know someone who has wandered, go looking for
the person. Have it out calmly, cleanly—but keep it between yourselves. If the wanderer listens, you have brought
a sister or a brother home. If they remain unbending, go
again—and this time not alone.

(Matthew 18:15–16)

**Scriptural
Reading**

Gracious God,
I'm thinking of three boors I know,
three loveless, joyless, gray-souled folk.
Now wait. I'm thinking . . .
All right, I have them fixed in my mind.
Now—how can I love them?
Not change them;
not remake them in my image. No.
How can I (tactfully) grace their lives?
Until I know, I will not say
A—n.

Closing

EVENING

Presence

Living God,
much that I hold dear
is deadly or dead.
Now, before I lose hold of my resolve,
prune them out of me.

Grace: God, give me the courage to be free.

Psalm 22

My God, my God! Why have you abandoned me?
I call all day, but you never hear or answer.
I am a worm they sidle past,
wagging their heads, jeering,
"Ha! If you're one of God's friends,
why doesn't God come and free you?"
And yet, was I deceived that I was your chosen?
I am the one you drew from the darkness,
through my mother's womb and into the light.
Then why have my heart and bones
melted like wax within me?
My mouth is drier than baked clay,
and my tongue clings to it like a leech.
I finger each of my ribs
as they cast lots for my clothes.
God, do not desert me to be savaged by these dogs.
You are God of the faint and failing.
And I am in need.

Closing

I Blesse thee, Lord, because I GROW
Among thy trees, which in a ROW
To thee both fruit and order OW.

What open force, or hidden CHARM
Can blast my fruit, or bring me HARM,
While the inclosure is thine ARM?

. . . .

When thou dost greater judgements SPARE,
And with thy knife but prune and PARE,
Ev'n fruitfull trees more fruitfull ARE.

Such sharpnes shows the sweetest FREND:
Such cuttings rather heal then REND:
And such beginnings touch their END.

(George Herbert, "Paradise")

Holy Friend,
the cocoon is always comfortable and warm—
and dull.
Crack my shell,
and send my spirit flying.
Make me see that dying is what the living do.
Amen.

Closing

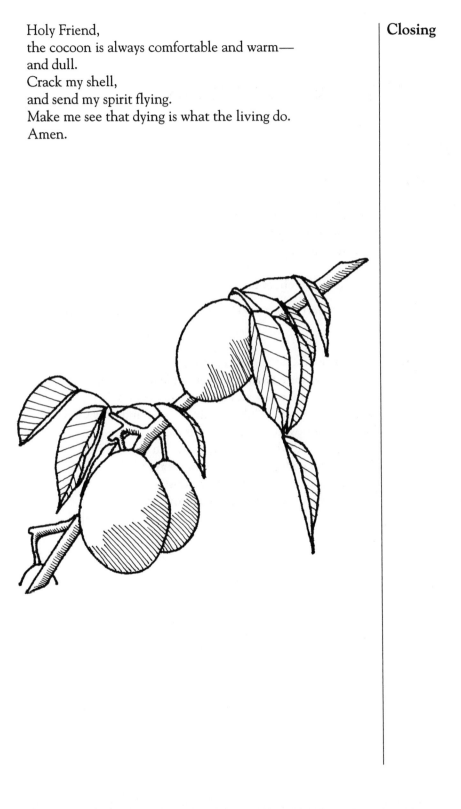

Second Friday

MORNING

Presence

Living God,
I am no longer a child.
~~You will not do my work,~~
play the game for me,
fight my battles.
So be it,
as long as you cheer me on the way.

Grace: God of surprises, when I am too content, disrupt
me.

Psalm

The voice of God came to me saying:
"Before you were born, I set you aside as my own.
I dedicated you to speak for me to all peoples."
"But," I stammered, "uh . . . uh . . . one and only God,
I know not how to speak. I'm but a child."
But God silenced me. "Do not say, 'I'm but a child.'
Rise up and go to those to whom I send you,
and bring them my message, fearlessly,
for I am with you to protect you from harm."

(Jeremiah 1:4–8)

I hearby swear to uphold your house
I would lay my bones in quick destroying lime
Or turn my flesh to timber for all time;
Cut down my womanhood; lop off the boughs
Of that perpetual ecstasy that grows
From the heart's core; condemn it as a crime
If it be broader than a beam, or climb
Above the stature that your roof allows.

I am not the hearthstone nor the cornerstone
Within this noble fabric you have builded;
Not by my beauty was its cornice gilded;
Not on my courage were its arches thrown:
My lord, adjudge my strength, and set me where
I bear a little more than I can bear.

(Elinor Wylie)

Hymn

God, my friend,
I offer you this day.
Let all my prayer, work, joy, suffering today
join with the lives offered to you
by the whole People of God
and especially with our great Eucharist,
Jesus,
your Son and our Brother.
Let your Spirit be with me today,
especially in . . .
And I ask your loving concern today,
especially for my friend . . .
Remind me, through the day, that I am not alone.
Amen.

Offering

DAYTIME

Presence | Living God,
the folk wisdom is filled with warnings:
keep your guard up,
beware of strangers,
don't get involved.
Let me laugh at them.

Grace: Shepherd of my soul, let me suffer like you, so that
I can heal like you.

Psalm | It was our suffering he bore on his back,
our sorrows, shortcomings, sins.
We scorned him as a felon, felled by God,
finally atoning for his endless, obstinate criticism.
But he was pierced in our place,
savaged for our silence,
scoffed at for our scorn.
And yet, in his wounds we are healed,
in his pain we find peace,
in his death we are born.

(Isaiah 53:4–5)

Hymn | Friendless and faint, with martyred steps and slow,
Faint for the flesh, but for the spirit free,
Stung by the mob that came to see the show,
The Master toiled along to Calvary;
We gibed him, as he went, with houndish glee,
Till his dimmed eyes for us did overflow;
We cursed his vengeless hands thrice wretchedly,—
And this was nineteen hundred years ago.

But after nineteen hundred years the shame
Still clings, and we have not made good the loss
That outraged faith had entered in his name.
Ah, when shall come love's courage to be strong!
Tell me, O Lord—tell me, O Lord, how long
Are we to keep Christ writhing on the cross!

(Edwin Arlington Robinson, "Calvary")

I don't mind my pain. It's their pain I can't stand. Let my pain go on and on, but stop theirs. Dear God, if only You could come down from Your cross for a while and let me get up there instead. If I could suffer like You, I could heal like You.

(Graham Greene, *The End of the Affair*)

Reading

There is no one of us—no matter what our race or sex or allegiance—who does not have the same blood and bones, the same flesh and frailty. So, too, the Christ. The Sanctifier must be of the same stock as the sanctified, so that by his death he might nullify Evil and his uncreation, death, to free us from our lifelong fear that death could sever us from God. For he did not pitch his tent among the disembodied angels but among the daughters and the sons of Abraham. He might become utterly at one with his sisters and brothers. Thus, our high priest has assumed all our weaknesses in every way; and thus he is trustworthy. He was defiled that he might expunge our defilement. He has survived all temptation to infidelity, and thus he can show us the way.

(Hebrews 2:14–18)

Scriptural Reading

God of life,
quiet my fears of the desert,
my misgivings of finding you there,
asking for more than I had planned.
Amen.

Closing

EVENING

Presence | Living God,
sleep is a little death
for each of which—
I have your word on it
—there is a resurrection.

Grace: God, let me use my days, not the other way round.

Psalm 90 | Eternal God,
to you a thousand years are a snap of the fingers.
You can brush your creation aside like a daydream.
We are like grass, dewy at dawn and dry before dusk.
Teach us to number the few days we have,
to count them like misers, aware of their worth,
knowing even the flawed, even the failures
are precious, because they are few.
Then we will be wise, waking gratefully,
gifted with one day more.

Because I could not stop for Death—
He kindly stopped for me—
The Carriage held but just Ourselves—
And Immortality.

We slowly drove—He knew no haste
And I had put away
My labor and my leisure too,
For His Civility—

We passed the School, where Children strove
At Recess—in the Ring—
We passed the Fields of Gazing Grain—
We passed the Setting Sun—

Or rather—He passed Us—
The Dews drew quivering and chill—
For only Gossamer, my Gown—
My Tippet—only Tulle—

We paused before a House that seemed
A Swelling of the Ground—
The Roof was scarcely visible—
The Cornice—in the Ground—

Since then—'tis Centuries—and yet
Feels shorter than the Day
I first surmised the Horses' Heads
Were toward Eternity—

(Emily Dickinson)

Holy Friend,
in this quiet moment, help me to know
that here—in this realm for which I was born—
there is no need of fear.
Amen.

Second Saturday

MORNING

Presence | Living God,
there is nothing today to make me run,
yet, inside, I'm already running.
Slow me down, so that I can see you now
and recognize you when we meet again today.

Grace: God, uproot my cowardly caution and cynicism.

Psalm | Beloved of God are the poor in spirit;
the joy of heaven is already theirs.
Beloved of God are the good-natured;
their soul already dwells in the land of promise.
Beloved of God are those for whom love brings sorrow;
they have been given the gift of consolation.
Beloved of God are those with a passion for honor;
their integrity ennobles all they meet.
Beloved of God are the compassionate and forgiving;
God will be compassionate and forgiving to them.
Beloved of God are the openhearted;
the Eternal dwells within them.
Beloved of God are those who mediate peace;
they are the sons and the daughters of God.
Beloved of God are those unbroken by their tormentors;
they dwell in God's house, now and forever.
(Matthew 5:3–10)

Thou shalt have one God only; who
Would be at the expense of two?
No graven images may be
Worshipped, except the currency:
Swear not at all; for thy curse
Thine enemy is none the worse:
At church on Sunday to attend
Will serve to keep the world thy friend:
Honour thy parents; that is, all
From whom advancement may befall:
Thou shalt not kill; but needst not strive
Officiously to keep alive:
Do not adultery commit;
Advantage rarely comes of it:
Thou shalt not steal; an empty feat,
When it's so lucrative to cheat:
Bear not false witness; let the lie
Have time on its own wings to fly:
Thou shalt not covet, but tradition
Approves all forms of competition.
      (Arthur Hugh Clough, "The Latest Decalogue")

Offering

God, my friend,
I offer you this day.
Let all my prayer, work, joy, suffering today
join with the lives offered to you
by the whole People of God
and especially with our great Eucharist,
Jesus,
your Son and our Brother.
Let your Spirit be with me today,
especially in . . .
And I ask your loving concern today,
especially for my friend . . .
Remind me, through the day, that I am not alone.
Amen.

DAYTIME

Presence

Living God,
I've spent years trying to grasp you,
hem you round,
box you into words.
But you are as elusive as love, truth, wisdom.
I will still strive to know about you.
But it's far important that I know you.

Grace: God, let me understand you not as a noun but a verb.

Psalm

In the beginning and always,
the Word—God's Wisdom—
was with him, was God,
from before the beginning.
From the well of God's being,
all things that are draw their "is."
Nothing that is came to be but through God.
What came to be in him was,
beyond mere existence: life,
a sharing in the being of God,
in the life which is light.
That light shines out in the surrounding darkness,
a light the darkness cannot overwhelm
or even grasp.

(John 1:1–5)

Hymn

Dear, secret greenness! nurst below
    Tempests and winds and winter nights!
Vex not, that but One sees thee grow;
    That One made all these lesser lights.

What needs a conscience calm and bright
    Within itself, an outward test?
Who breaks his glass, to take more light,
    Makes way for storms into his rest.

Then bless thy secret growth, nor catch
    At noise, but thrive unseen and dumb;
Keep clean, bear fruit, earn life, and watch
    Till the white-winged reapers come!
      (Henry Vaughan, "The Seed Growing Secretly")

To proportion one's task to one's powers, to undertake to speak only when one knows, not to force oneself to think what one does not think, or to understand what one does not understand,—to avoid the danger of missing the substance of things and disguising its absence under big words: all that is great wisdom. Pride rebels against it; but pride is the enemy.

(A. D. Sertillanges, *The Intellectual Life*)

Reading

The message that the cross embodies seems foolishness to those who hold themselves aloof from it, who regard whatever surpasses their understanding as foolish. But for those of us who sense its inner truth, it is the power of God to unblind us. As Scripture says, "I will confound the wisdom of the worldly-wise and defy the erudition of the clever." Today, our own great modern thinkers are abashed before the wisdom of God, as were the ancient Jewish scholars and the Greek philosophers. The Jews wanted miraculous deliverance; the Greeks wanted ultimate proof. And here we preach a crucified Christ! A scandal. To the Jews, a dead end; to the Greeks, gibberish. We believe not because we called God and God answered our expectations, but because God calls us and we answer. To us, Jesus is the Christ, the wisdom and power of God, whose foolishness is more subtle than human wisdom and whose weakness is more compelling than human power.

(1 Corinthians 1:18–25)

Scriptural Reading

Faithful God,
only pain pushes us to think,
and thought makes us wise,
and wisdom sets us free.
Worth the cost!
Amen.

Closing

EVENING

Presence

Living God,
I pause, at peace,
distanced on both sides
from the bustle of the week.
May I be silent and let you speak.

Grace: God, let me own the truth: that you accept me.

Psalm

What's left to say?
If God is with us, who is really against us?
If God did not spare the Son,
but surrendered him that we might truly live,
how does God judge our worth?
What can intrude between Christ's love and us?
Not troubles, torment, threats;
they are the trials through which we triumph, as did he.
No, no. There is nothing! I'm certain.
Neither death nor life, no power of earth or heaven,
nothing now or yet to come,
no unearthly power nor any created thing
can separate us from the love of God—
made visible among us in Jesus the Christ.

(Romans 8:31–39)

Hymn

At once a voice arose among
    The bleak twigs overhead
In full-hearted evensong
    Of joy illimited;
An aged thrush, frail, gaunt, and small,
    In blast-beruffled plume,
Had chosen thus to fling his soul
    Upon the growing gloom.

So little cause for carolings
    Of such ecstatic sound
Was written on terrestrial things
    Afar or nigh around,
That I could think there trembled through
    His happy good-night air
Some blessed Hope, whereof he knew
    And I was unaware.

(Thomas Hardy, "The Darkling Thrush")

Holy Friend,
I grasp the hope you hold out to me
in both my hands
and leap.
Amen.

Closing

❧ Third Week ❧

Third Sunday

MORNING

Presence

Living God,
the wilderness I paw my way through daily
is really no blasted heath or empty sea of sand.
My days have landmarks, benchmarks, goals.
But in this otherwhere,
I am lost
unless you take my hand.

Grace: God, if there is nobility in serving, let me feel it.

Psalm

John, the baptizer, speaks:
"The bride is not for me. She is for the Bridegroom.
I am his friend. I stand and await his will.
Ah, how my heart quickens when he speaks.
His joy infects me, his love for her.
I am born of earth; he, of God.
I am not the Prince. I am his attendant lord.
His words, heeded, give eternal life.
How graced I am that I do not crave his place.
How wretched I would be if I were Lord!"

(John 3:29–36)

He, of his gentleness,
Thirsting and hungering
Walked in the wilderness;
Soft words of grace he spoke
Unto lost desert-folk
That listened wondering. . . .
Comrade, with ragged coat,
Gaunt ribs—poor innocent—
Bleeding foot, burning throat,
The guileless young scapegoat:
For forty nights and days
Followed in Jesus' ways,
Sure guard behind him kept,
Tears like a lover wept.

(Robert Graves, "In the Wilderness")

Hymn

God, my friend,
I offer you this day.
Let all my prayer, work, joy, suffering today
join with the lives offered to you
by the whole People of God
and especially with our great Eucharist,
Jesus,
your Son and our Brother.
Let your Spirit be with me today,
especially in . . .
And I ask your loving concern today,
especially for my friend . . .
Remind me, through the day, that I am not alone.
Amen.

Offering

DAYTIME

Presence | Living God,
I can kid myself.
I can kid anyone I meet.
Not you.

Grace: God, let me live for one epitaph: honest.

Psalm 49 | I cannot redeem myself nor pay my ransom to God.
Who could pay the price, cover the cost
for . . . everything?

I will write you, my God, a psalm; I will sing you a song!
Poor, loving lackwit that I am.
The wise and the learned—the word-wielders—die.
Their graves are no deeper, wider, longer
than the fool's.
The wise one's books, the world-beater's fortune
go to someone else.
Who enters their monumental tomes or tombs?
There is but one legacy: the joy you've left behind.
Listen! Hear!

Hymn | Be near me when my light is low,
When the blood creeps, and the nerves prick
And tingle; and the heart is sick,
And all the wheels of being slow.

Be near me when the sensuous frame
Is rack'd with pangs that conquer trust;
And Time, a maniac scattering dust,
And Life, a Fury slinging flame.

Be near me when my faith is dry,
And men the flies of latter spring,
That lay their eggs, and sting and sing
And weave their petty cells and die.

Be near me when I fade away,
To point the term of human strife,
And on the low dark verge of life
The twilight of eternal day.

(Alfred Lord Tennyson, "In Memoriam")

It is very different for the nasty people—the little, low, timid, warped, thin-blooded, lonely people, or the passionate, sensual, unbalanced people. If they make any attempt at goodness at all, they learn, in double quick time, that they need help. It is Christ or nothing for them. It is taking up the cross and following—or else despair.

(C. S. Lewis, *Mere Christianity*)

Reading

There seems to be a principle here, a pattern in my life. Every single time—almost without fail—when I want to do good, I end up doing evil. In the depths of me, truly, my spirit delights in walking the way God asks. My mind sees that noble ideal and hears God's voice. But there is another voice, the voice of my flesh, which wields a whip and points the other way. I am a prisoner between these two voices.

My God, what a wretch! Who can rescue me from this striving, anchored self?

Thank God! It is done! In Jesus, the Christ!

This I—who serves my weakness in sin—is strong enough to rule myself and serve my God.

(Romans 7:21–25)

Scriptural Reading

Saving God,
I catch myself being condescending
to the Jews of Jesus' time,
when he came to them
and they failed to see you in him,
found him only an irritation,
tolerable—to a point.
Odd. I rarely realize that I do exactly the same
when he comes disguised to me.
We both know the times I mean.
Amen.

Closing

EVENING

Presence | Living God,
let the day settle.
Becalm me.
Peace.

Grace: God, unburden me of my grudges, and thus make
my life simpler.

Psalm | Child, be gentle as you go about your business.
The greater you are, the more noblesse oblige,
for our God—unspeakably great—waits on us
and will not enter your house unasked.
Be humble, too, before the great unanswered questions.
They are the infinite sea that you will never cross.
Float there; rejoice that there is always more.
When you are modified before the truth,
you are not less;
you are far more able to forgive.

(Ecclesiasticus 3:17–24)

Hymn | Thy God hath not denied thee all,
Whilst he permits thee but to call.
Call to thy God for grace to keep
Thy vows; and if thou break them, weep.
Weep for thy broken vows, and vow again:
Vows made with tears cannot be still in vain.
Then once again
I vow to mend my ways;
Lord, say Amen,
And thine be all the praise.

(George Herbert, "Said I Not So?")

Holy Friend,
all of them are callous to my pain,
my need,
my fumbled intentions.
(As I, of course, am callous to theirs.)
Amen.

Closing

Third Monday

Presence

Living God,
after the two days' retreat
from all the petty skirmishes,
while you allowed me to relent,
remind me where I come from
and whereunto I'm sent.

Grace: Holy Friend, remind me why you gave my heart a
voice.

Psalm 101

O God, I'm not blameless. I can only strive.
Let me go forward with an unsullied heart,
quick, not just to see, but
to declare injustice,
less afraid of what the hard of heart have to say
than of what my shaming silence would say of me.
It is as easy to ignore hypocrisy and lies
as to pass the battered victim in the ditch,
going my righteous way unsoiled and neuter.
If they are free to speak, then so am I.
Surely, I'll not prevail while I'm alive,
but I will do far more than merely to survive.

Hymn

All I have is a voice
To undo the folded lie,
The romantic lie in the brain
Of the sensual man-in-the-street
And the lie of Authority
Whose buildings grope the sky:
There is no such thing as the State
And no one exists alone;
Hunger allows no choice
To the citizen or the police;
We must love one another or die.

(W. H. Auden, "The Unknown Citizen")

God, my friend,
I offer you this day.
Let all my prayer, work, joy, suffering today
join with the lives offered to you
by the whole People of God
and especially with our great Eucharist,
Jesus,
your Son and our Brother.
Let your Spirit be with me today,
especially in . . .
And I ask your loving concern today,
especially for my friend . . .
Remind me, through the day, that I am not alone.
Amen.

Offering

🌿

DAYTIME

Living God,
wisdom is born of humility,
and humility springs from truth.

Presence

Grace: God, if I am gifted, let me remember they are gifts.

All you with power of judgment on the earth,
before you judge, betake yourselves to God
and reflect with humble heart upon God's ways.
God is just and will not be swayed by guile,
nor taken in by stratagems and craft.
The judgments of God test one thing: truth.
Your quest for truth, then, asks for nimble wits
and more, far more: God's Wisdom in your heart.
That Wisdom is the Spirit of God,
which reads the human heart and not mere words.
No book of law can ever capture holy Wisdom,
and those in whom Wisdom dwells may use the gift well,
but never pass that gift to someone else.
Like God's justice, Wisdom cannot be bought.
There is only one place Wisdom may be sought:
in your silent soul, before the feet of God.

(Wisdom 1:1–8)

Psalm

Hymn

I met a traveller from an antique land
Who said: Two vast and trunkless legs of stone
Stand in the desert . . . Near them, on the sand,
Half sunk, a shattered visage lies, whose frown,
And wrinkled lip, and sneer of cold command,
Tell that its sculptor well those passions read
Which yet survive, stamped on these lifeless things,
The hand that mocked them, and the heart that fed:
And on the pedestal these words appear:
"My name is Ozymandias, king of kings:
Look on my works, ye Mighty, and despair!"
Nothing beside remains. Round the decay
Of that colossal wreck, boundless and bare
The lone and level sands stretch far away.
(Percy Bysshe Shelley, "Ozymandias")

Reading

A prayer to the Magi, by Helena, mother of the Emperor
Constantine:

"Like me, . . . you were late in coming. . . . For you the
primordial discipline of the heavens was relaxed and a new
defiant light blazed amid the disconcerted stars.

"How laboriously you came, taking sights and calculating. . . . How odd you looked on the road, . . . laden
with such preposterous gifts!

"Yet you came, and were not turned away. . . . Your
gifts were not needed, but they were accepted and put
carefully by, for they were brought with love. . . .

"Dear cousins, pray for me. . . .

"For His sake who did not reject your curious gifts, pray
always for all the learned, the oblique, the delicate. Let
them not be quite forgotten at the Throne of God when
the simple come into their kingdom."
(Evelyn Waugh, *Helena*)

In the town of Jericho, there lived a runty little chap named Zacchaeus, whose dismissable stature was not the only burden he bore. You see, in a town where most folks' bellies howled all day, Zacchaeus was very, very rich. What's more, he had amassed his wealth by skimming the taxes of the very folks whose bellies were bellowing. He was not popular.

Scriptural Reading

One day, Zacchaeus heard that Jesus was walking through the town, and he was anxious to see what kind of man this famous fellow was. But the streets were thronged with people, and Zacchaeus trotted along behind their backs, jumping up and trying to catch a glimpse, to no avail. But Zacchaeus hadn't become chief tax collector by sitting on his wits, so he climbed a sycamore tree and peered down at the procession.

Just as Jesus got to the sycamore, he stopped and grinned up at the startled little man peering down through the leaves. "Zacchaeus," he said, "come down. Hurry. I must rest in your home today."

As the little fellow came shinnying down, the hungrier and therefore more worthy citizens sniffed, "Well! He's going to stay with a sinner!"

But Zacchaeus stood his ground. "Look, sir," he said, treading on his own toes, "I will give half my property to the poor. If . . . I have cheated anybody, I'll . . . pay them back . . . four times over."

Jesus smiled at him. "Today," he said, "salvation has come to stay in your home."

(Luke 19:1–10)

Holy Friend,
I know the truth,
that appearances deceive;
that the point is not poverty or plenty,
talents of gold or talents of the soul,
only the readiness of the heart.
Remind me that merely knowing that
is not enough.
Amen.

Closing

EVENING

Presence | Living God,
before I stow the day away,
rest with me here awhile,
so that the day can coalesce
into a seamless peace.

Grace: God of all goodness, let me come to you first, not
just after I've lost the way.

Psalm 16 | How wonderful are your gifts to me;
how good you are!
You have shown me the landmarks,
my guide, my teacher, my friend.
With you at my side, I cannot fail.
So my heart and soul exult.
I stride on confidently.
You have only to point out the path.

Hymn | My Soul, there is a countrie
    Afar beyond the stars,
Where stands a winged Sentrie
    All skilful in the wars.
There, above noise and danger,
    Sweet peace sits, crown'd with smiles,
And One born in a manger
    Commands the beauteous files.
He is thy gracious friend
    And (O my Soul awake!)
Did in pure love descend,
    To die here for thy sake.
If thou canst get but thither,
    There growes the flowre of peace,
The rose that cannot wither,
    Thy fortresse, and thy ease.
Leave then thy foolish ranges;
    For none can thee secure,
But One, who never changes,
    Thy God, thy Life, thy Cure.

(Henry Vaughan, "Peace")

Holy Friend,
you made me restless,
so that I would search you out.
Now that I have found you
(or, rather, the other way round),
let me rest awhile.
Amen.

Closing

Third Tuesday

Presence Living God,
I see things fairly clearly
in these quiet moments alone with you.
But the day begins,
and all the assaulting voices conspire,
claiming my allegiance
or at least my quiet connivance.

Grace: God, don't let me take for truth what I know is
trash.

Psalm Before Christ found me, I was fumbling in the dark;
the lights I trusted led me away from him.
Now I see that anything outside Jesus is loss.
For him, glad-heartedly, I give up everything;
it is all well lost, when Christ can be my wealth.
Before, I thought observance of the law
enough, that I could justify myself.
I put my faith in me and not in God.
But it is the resurrected Christ who frees my power,
transforms me, lifts my life into God's.
To share his rising I must share his suffering.
I am not perfect yet; I have not won.
I am still running, trying to capture the prize
for which Christ captured me.

(Philippians 3:7–14)

That glorious Form, that Light unsufferable,
And that far-beaming blaze of Majesty,
Wherewith he wont at Heav'ns high Councel-Table,
To sit the midst of Trinal Unity,
He laid aside; and here with us to be,
    Forsook the Courts of everlasting Day,
And chose with us a darksom House of mortal Clay.
    (John Milton, "On the Morning of Christ's Nativity")

God, my friend,
I offer you this day.
Let all my prayer, work, joy, suffering today
join with the lives offered to you
by the whole People of God
and especially with our great Eucharist,
Jesus,
your Son and our Brother.
Let your Spirit be with me today,
especially in . . .
And I ask your loving concern today,
especially for my friend . . .
Remind me, through the day, that I am not alone.
Amen.

Hymn

Offering

DAYTIME

Presence

Living God,
at the Incarnation,
your Word took on himself
what you had never known before
except from the outside:
vulnerability,
woundedness,
doubt.
Welcome.

Grace: God, your Son stripped himself of your powers;
strip me of my pretensions to them.

Psalm

He was one with God and shared God's power,
but he did not clutch it like a miser's prize:
the equality of his glory with God.
Instead, he emptied himself,
not of his Godness but of its gifts,
to take on the powerlessness of a slave.
He became as we are, and humbler yet,
he even accepted death with us,
the ultimate death of the cross.
For that, God has raised him back up,
above the loftiest heights,
and returned to him the unspeakable Name,
so that everything that is should bend the knee
and cry aloud to the glory of God
that Jesus is the Christ.

(Philippians 2:6–11)

Hymn

no time ago
or else a life
walking in the dark
i met christ

jesus)my heart
flopped over
and lay still
while he passed(as

close as i'm to you
yes closer
made of nothing
except loneliness

(e. e. cummings)

Reading

During the war, a British friend of Madeleine L'Engle lost her husband and her three small children in an air raid. For the rest of the war, she worked for the destitute, doing "her passionate grieving in private." Later she fell in love again with a man who asked her to marry him and begin a family again. She knew the awful risk. "But she made the dangerous decision. She dared to love again."

Years later, L'Engle told the story at a college, "and during a reception a handsome young philosophy professor came up to me; she had been married and her husband had died; she told me that she was not going to do as the Englishwoman had done; she was never going to open herself to that kind of pain again; she refused to be vulnerable.

"I do not think that I would want to be a student in her philosophy classes."

(Madeleine L'Engle, *Walking on Water*)

Scriptural Reading

Jesus came to his own home. And his own people treated him like an alien. But not all. And those who did take him in, he empowered to become children of God—born not out of some human potential, not out of some fleshly urge, not from some human will to possess divinity. No, they were reborn of God.

The Word became one with our flesh, and pitched his tent among us.

(John 1:9–14)

Closing

Holy God,
my total self-reliance
not only renders you helpless,
but enfeebles me as well.
I am far more useful in your hands
than in my own.
Amen.

EVENING

Presence | Living God,
I've had pretensions, as I said,
to your position—
to the unquestionable power,
the independence,
the control.
But when I think of you
embodied in the Christ,
I have salutary second thoughts.

Grace: God, help me grasp how vulnerable you must be to
have consented to create us.

Psalm | We have been graced by Jesus to make his glory ours.
And this is not all we humbly boast.
We declare our pride in facing hardship.
Enduring suffering makes us steadfast,
and in steadfastness we anchor our dignity,
and our dignity is the armor of our hope.
Not that we purchase pride of God's esteem with pain.
Our boast is that we have been chosen;
our pride is to share the lot of the Crucified;
our glory is not our love for God,
but the outpouring of God's love on our unworthiness.
We were helpless, hopeless, undeserving,
but in spite of that, God yielded us the Son, Jesus.
What kind of obstinate love is that!

(Romans 5:2–11)

He cried no cry when they drave the nails

And the blood gushed hot and free,
The hounds of the crimson sky gave tongue
But never a cry cried he.

I ha' seen him cow a thousand men
On the hills o' Galilee,
They whined as he walked out calm between,
Wi' his eyes like the grey o' the sea.

Like the sea that brooks no voyaging
With the winds unleashed and free,
Like the sea that he cowed at Genseret
Wi' twey words spoke' suddently.

A master of men was the Goodly Fere.*
A mate of the wind and sea,
if they think they ha' slain our Goodly Fere
They are fools eternally.

I ha' seen him eat o' the honey-comb
Sin' they nailed him to the tree.
                    (Ezra Pound, "Ballad of the Goodly Fere")

Holy Friend,

Closing

my heart grasps what is too slippery for my mind:
faithfulness to the faithless,
clinging doggedly to hope,
loving the relentlessly unlovely.
At times, I thought it was perverse.
Now, I wonder if it is the way
to be like you.
Amen.

*Fere=Mate, Companion

Third Wednesday

Presence

Living God,
there are so many people and places I hold precious.
If you were to ask me to surrender them,
my heart would most likely crumble.
But I've come to realize
that my heart is not my soul.

Grace: Love, stretch my perspective, at least in the
direction of yours.

Psalm

Abraham took the wood and laid it on Isaac, his beloved.
But he kept the fire in his own hands. And the knife.
"Father," the boy said, "here are the fire and wood.
But where is the lamb to be slain and offered?"
And the old man said, "Son, God has provided it."
When they arrived at the place that God had pointed out,
Abraham built the altar and arranged the wood.
Then he bound Isaac, his beloved, God's promised gift,
and laid him on the wood and raised the knife to slay him.
"Wait!" cried the voice of God. "Enough! Enough!
Don't raise your hand against the boy or harm him.
You know now that your trust in me is secure;
you know that Isaac is Isaac and God is God."
And Abraham looked up and saw a ram caught
by the curl of its horns in the gnarls of a thornbush.
And he sacrificed the ram in place of his only son.

(Genesis 22:1–13)

Trust me, I have not earned your dear rebuke,—
    I love, as you would have me, God the most;
    Would lose not Him, but you, must one be lost,
Nor with Lot's wife cast back a faithless look,
Unready to forego what I forsook;
      This say I, having counted up the cost,
      This, though I be the feeblest of God's host,
The sorriest sheep Christ shepherds with His crook.
Yet while I love my God the most, I deem
      That I can never love you overmuch;
        I love Him more, so let me love you too;
      Yea, as I apprehend it, love is such
I cannot love you if I love not Him,
        I cannot love Him if I love not you.
      (Christina Georgina Rossetti, "Monna Innominata")

Offering

God, my friend,
I offer you this day.
Let all my prayer, work, joy, suffering today
join with the lives offered to you
by the whole People of God
and especially with our great Eucharist,
Jesus,
your Son and our Brother.
Let your Spirit be with me today,
especially in . . .
And I ask your loving concern today,
especially for my friend . . .
Remind me, through the day, that I am not alone.
Amen.

DAYTIME

Presence | Living God,
you know every movement of my mind,
even what is smeared to me
is clear to you.
But I grope for your intentions
like one blind.
You have sent me on this quest for you.
I cannot find you by myself.

Grace: God, it is so difficult not to be in control; purge
me of the craving.

Psalm | Again, God speaks to Job, the battler:
"Have you ever in your life commanded the sunrise
or sent the dawn to grasp the earth by its edges?
Have you walked the dark abysses of the sea?
If you know them as I do, I will hear your counsel.
Have you plowed to the place where the snow is stored?
Can you grasp the fiery forks of lightning in your hands
or cavort among the stars with Orion and the Bear?
At your approach, does all that is cry out, 'Here we are!'
You, who would have me yield my place: speak."

(Job 38:12–35)

Hymn and Reading | The big black Lab galumphs beside me as I walk,
tongue lolling, eyes intent upon the stick.
He's submissive to my whistle, not my trifling talk,
nor well-wrought reasons, much less rhetoric.
He trots ahead and turns, impatient for the throw,
snaps off a bark, then lumbers halfway back.
He cocks his head and huffs to tell me I'm too slow.
I throw and off he goes, a blur of black.
The world exists for him: the stick, the roadside, me.
We're here to serve his simple solipsism.
Except for unpredictable caprice, he's free,
without the humbling need for baptism.

To save him from a truck, I choke his collar short.
What earthly link? That noise, this loss of breath?
He punctuates his protest with a snort;
until they meet, no need to ponder death.
What a narrow scope of truth his mind explores:
betrayal, hunger, curiosity.
He knows my mind about as I do yours;
my thoughts as closed to him as yours to me.
How humbling to confront one's hubris, open-eyed,
to fathom what this big black mongrel feels.
I'd thought that you and I were striding side by side,
when all the time I was galumphing at your heels.

Scriptural Reading

Our knowledge of God is always as inadequate as our pre-
dictions of the future. But once we are fulfilled, how can
there be anything inadequate in us again? When I was a
child, I used to talk, think, argue like a child—who has
just enough grasp of the truth to be thoroughly confused.
When I grew up, I was somewhat better than that, but
hardly perfect. I still see God through a smear of distorting
glass. Ah! but then we will see God face-to-face! Now I
know God so incompletely; then, I will know God through
and through, as God knows me now.

(1 Corinthians 13:8–12)

Closing

Immortal Friend,
imperfection is a gift
which no animal or angel was given.
Let me rejoice in it, then,
that alone among all your creatures
I am always capable of more.
Amen.

EVENING

Presence | Living God,
what can I give in return
for your brightening all darkness,
dignifying my pain,
rescuing me from meaninglessness?
Ask.

Grace: God of all truth, let me be content and proud of
what I've done today, but not too content or proud.

Psalm 34 | God, how good you are! I can taste you with my soul!
You are a warm shelter in the storm.
Those who stand in awe of you are whole.
Fulfillment is not found in fame,
or power, or flesh, or length of days.
The path to peace is peacemaking;
the flesh is to serve the soul;
and the soul is to seek more life.
Oh, virtue knows hardship, too—
most likely better than the vicious do.
But there is the secret of you, God:
that hardship is the climb to you.

Look at the stars! look, look up at the skies!
   O look at all the fire-folk sitting in the air!
   The bright boroughs, the circle-citadels there!
Down in the dim woods the diamond delves! the
      elves'-eyes!

The grey lawns cold where gold, where quickgold lies!
   Wind-beat whitebeam! airy abeles set on a flare!
   Flake-doves sent floating forth at a farmyard scare!—
Ah well! it is all a purchase, all is a prize.

Buy then! bid then!—What?—Prayer, patience, alms,
      vows.
Look, look: a May-mess, like on orchard boughs!
   Look! March-bloom, like on mealed-with-yellow
      sallows!
These are indeed the barn; withindoors house
The shocks. This piece-bright paling shuts the spouse
   Christ home, Christ and his mother and all his hallows.
      (Gerard Manley Hopkins, "The Starlight Night")

Hymn

Holy Friend,
you are there,
pulsing under all the surfaces,
beyond the reach of my eyes,
but not the reach of my soul.
Amen.

Closing

Third Thursday

MORNING

Presence

Living God,
sometimes when I open myself to you,
I fear I may be talking to myself.
At those times, make me remember
the humbling trust of children,
how my body heals itself,
the miracle of my eyes,
so that I may realize
how foolish that fear is.

Grace: God, let the core of my confidence be my faith in
you.

Psalm 33

God, your word is what integrity means:
dependable, loving, creative.
Your presence is the spark of justice,
igniting the just to strive.
By the breath of your mouth the land arose,
and you brushed back the seas with your hand.
How then will the hard-hearted resist you?
We stand behind your shield, O God,
relentless, patient, faithful one.
Who can withstand us forever?

Hymn

Morning has broken
like the first morning,
Blackbird has spoken
like the first bird.
Praise for the singing!
Praise for the morning! . . .
God's re-creation of the new day!
      (Eleanor Farjeon, "Morning Has Broken")

God, my friend,
I offer you this day.
Let all my prayer, work, joy, suffering today
join with the lives offered to you
by the whole People of God
and especially with our great Eucharist,
Jesus,
your Son and our Brother.
Let your Spirit be with me today,
especially in . . .
And I ask your loving concern today,
especially for my friend . . .
Remind me, through the day, that I am not alone.
Amen.

Offering

DAYTIME

Presence | Living God,
I am what I am;
there's no escaping that.
Why do I keep trying?

Grace: God, let me be grateful for who I am.

Psalm | Poverty or plenty is not the point.
I have learned to manage on whatever I have.
I know how to be poor, and I don't mind being rich.
Neither my want nor my wealth can get in my way.
I'm no novice anymore, and I am whetted, ready—
full belly or empty, poverty or plenty—
for anything, anywhere.
There is nothing I cannot do now—nothing—
with the help of the One who strengthens me.
(Philippians 4:11–20)

Hymn | As kingfishers catch fire, dragonflies draw flame;
As tumbled over rim in roundy wells
Stones ring; like each tucked string tells, each hung bell's
Bow swung finds tongue to fling out broad its name;
Each mortal thing does one thing and the same:
Deals out that being indoors each one dwells;
Selves—goes itself; *myself* it speaks and spells;
Crying *What I do is me: for that I came.*

I say more: the just man justices;
Keeps grace: that keeps all his goings graces;
Acts in God's eye what in God's eye he is—
Christ—for Christ plays in ten thousand places,
Lovely in limbs, and lovely in eyes not his
To the Father through the features of men's faces.
(Gerard Manley Hopkins)

"I remember seeing a Punch and Judy show when I was a child. Punch had hidden his money in an earthenware pot and he was waving his arms about at the other side of the stage so the policeman might not notice it. I think you are always waving your arms to prevent other people from seeing the reality of you, or perhaps to hide it from yourself."

(Georges Bernanos, *The Diary of a Country Priest*)

Moses said, "Uh, my God, I . . . I never in my life have been what you'd call . . . uh . . . eloquent. Never. I mean . . . even after our little talks together. You see, I . . . I . . . stammer, you see. I do- . . . don't speak well at all."

"Hm," God mused. "Where do you suppose a mouth comes from? Who would you guess makes this one speechless and that one deaf? This one clear-eyed and that one blind?"

"Uh, you, God. But . . . if . . . if . . . if it would please you, there . . . must be someone else."

"Hm," God mused again. "Yes. Yes, I suppose I had better go with you."

(Exodus 4:10–13)

Living Light,
let me stop making apologies and excuses
and get on with it.
Amen.

Reading

Scriptural Reading

Closing

EVENING

Presence | Living God,
you kindle life in the unlikeliest places.
I'm surely dry tinder now.
Try me.

Grace: God, I am only a supplement to you; let me be a
worthy one.

Psalm 143 | All those who prize our God, sing praise,
from horizon to horizon, from the heart to heaven.
The Timeless-Transcendent is in our midst.
You haunt the ghettos, the ash heaps, and the gutters.
You search for the lame, the pariahs, and the lost.
All those who are no ones are yours.
And you will raise them up from the depths
as you raised your Anointed from death,
and you will crown them the peers of your Realm.

Hymn | And if tonight my soul may find her peace
in sleep, and sink in good oblivion,
and in the morning wake like a new-opened flower
then I have been dipped again in God, and new-created.

And if, as weeks go round, in the dark of the moon
my spirit darkens and goes out, and soft strange gloom
pervades my movements and my thoughts and words
then I shall know that I am walking still
with God, we are close together now the moon's in
shadow. . . .
then I must know that still
I am in the hands [of] the unknown God,
he is breaking me down to his own oblivion
to send me forth on a new morning, a new man.
(D. H. Lawrence, "Shadows")

Holy Friend,
I am in your hands.
Whatever awaits us tomorrow,
we can cope with then.
Amen.

Closing

Third Friday

Presence

Living God,
you create no hunger
for which there is no food,
and only you can nourish the hunger of my soul.

Grace: God, let me follow with good grace.

Psalm 42

As the doe searches the wood for running streams,
so my soul roams in search of you, the living God.
You raised in me this stubborn thirst for life,
and nothing you've made can slake it; only you.
Deep cries out to deep to seduce me from the path,
cataracts of promises to lure me off the way.
But I set my footsteps steadfast where you've walked,
and in the going I fulfill your will for me,
for I go to the altar of God,
to God who gave joy to my youth.

Who in this Bowling Alley bowld the Sun?
Who made it always when it rises set
To go at once both down, and up to get?
Who th'Curtain rods made for this Tapistry?
Who hung the twinckling Lanthorns in the Sky?
Who? who did this? or who is he? Why, know
Its Onely Might Almighty this did doe.
His hand hath made this noble worke which Stands
His Glorious Handywork not made by hands.
Who spake all things from nothing; and with ease
Can speake all things to nothing, if he please. . . .
Oh! what a might is this Whose single frown
Doth shake the world as it would shake it down?
Which All from Nothing fet,* from Nothing, All:
Hath All on Nothing set, lets Nothing fall.
Gave All to nothing Man indeed, whereby
Through nothing man all might him Glorify.

(Edward Taylor)

Hymn

God, my friend,
I offer you this day.
Let all my prayer, work, joy, suffering today
join with the lives offered to you
by the whole People of God
and especially with our great Eucharist,
Jesus,
your Son and our Brother.
Let your Spirit be with me today,
especially in . . .
And I ask your loving concern today,
especially for my friend . . .
Remind me, through the day, that I am not alone.
Amen.

Offering

*fet=made

DAYTIME

Presence

Living God,
for a long time
I tried to bribe you with my goodness
then to bargain with promises for reprieves,
bartering my soul with you
instead of surrendering what was already yours.

Grace: God, rid me of my fear of loss.

Psalm

God, you have gifted me with a disciple's tongue,
so that, since I have learned, I now may teach.
Each morning you bid me listen, then send me forth
to speak to my people whom I love.
Even so, in their wickedness and rebellion,
they fall on me and beat me for an interfering fool.
For my part, I stand with my fists at my sides.
I offer myself to the lash of their insults;
I face down their sneering, the curses, their spittle.
I set my jaw like flint, and I am untroubled.
For you are my vindicator.
You will melt their malice
like a cloak devoured by moths.

(Isaiah 50:4–9)

Hymn

Lord, who createdst man in wealth and store,
    Though foolishly he lost the same,
        Decaying more and more,
           Till he became
              Most poore:
              With thee
           O let me rise
        As larks, harmoniously,
    And sing this day thy victories:
Then shall the fall further the flight in me.

(George Herbert, "Easter-wings")

Christ says "Give me All. I don't want so much of your
time and so much of your money and so much of your
work: I want You. . . . No half-measures are any good. I
don't want to cut off a branch here and a branch there, I
want to have the whole tree down. . . . Hand over the
whole natural self, all the desires which you think innocent
as well as the ones you think wicked—the whole outfit. I
will give you a new self instead. In fact, I will give you
Myself: my own will shall become yours."

(C. S. Lewis, Mere Christianity)

Reading

One day during the time of searing drought, the prophet
Elijah came to the town of Zarephath, and at the gate he
saw a gaunt woman gathering sticks. "Please," he said, "I'm
thirsty. Could you give me a little water?" The woman
looked at him, puzzled, but turned toward her house to get
him a drink. "And please," Elijah called after her, "a scrap
of bread?" The woman sighed. "Sir," she said, "by the God
you believe in, I have no bread, only a handful of meal in
the jar and a bit of oil in the jug. When you came along, I
was gathering a few sticks to make a last meal for myself
and my little boy. Then we shall die."

"Please," Elijah said, "in the name of God."

So the woman went and did as Elijah asked and shared
all she had left in the world with him and with her son.
And from that moment, every day, when the woman went
to her jar of meal and her jug of oil, they were full once
again.

(1 Kings 17:7–16)

Scriptural Reading

Holy Friend,
love costs
and costs more when it's freely given,
and each impoverishment
enriches me.
Amen.

Closing

EVENING

Presence | Living God,
I live hemmed in by mirrors.
Upbraiding my lack of progress, power, popularity,
success, sex, security—
the lot.
Shatter the mirrors.

Grace: God, let me put my sins behind me, and myself
with them.

Psalm 51 | Have mercy on me, all-knowing God, in your goodness,
absorbing my failures in your fathomless compassion.
I'm far too well aware of my faults;
I would be glad for judgment, to be purged of them,
so that you and I can leave my sins behind us and get on.
Uproot my guilt and sow my soul with joy—with you—
so my life is filled with you and not myself.

Hymn | This day, be bread and peace my lot:
    All else beneath the sun,
Thou know'st if best bestowed or not;
    And let Thy will be done.

To Thee, whose temple is all space,
    Whose altar, earth, sea, skies,
One chorus let all being raise;
    All nature's incense rise!
                (Alexander Pope, "The Universal Prayer")

Holy Friend,
give me the final, best gift:
to look at my peccadillos as I do those of my friends
and say, "So what?
We're still friends."
And laugh.
Amen.

Closing

Third Saturday

MORNING

Presence | Living God,
all week long I've worked at what you asked:
shepherding in your place.
Now, I need no small shepherding myself.

Grace: God, whet my senses to the magic you do in plain
sight.

Psalm 147 | How good it feels to sing your glory, my God!
You count out the stars, one by one, and name them.
If you care so much for flecks of fire in the night,
ah! how much more for us, who will outlast the stars!
You herd the clouds of heaven to send down rain,
and boil mellow fruitfulness up into the land.
You feed cattle and birds when they cry their need.
You need no battalions of workers; just your word.
You are our shepherd too. We shall not want.

Hymn | O Earth! thou hast not any wind that blows
Which is not music; every weed of thine
Pressed rightly flows in aromatic wine;
And every humble hedgerow flower that grows,
And every little brown bird that doth sing,
Hath something greater than itself, and bears
A living Word to every living thing,
Albeit it hold the Message unawares.
All shapes and sounds have something which is not
Of them: a Spirit broods amid the grass;
Vague outlines of the Everlasting Thought
Lie in the melting shadows as they pass;
The touch of an Eternal Presence thrills
The fringes of the sunsets and the hills.

(Richard Realf, "The World")

God, my friend,
I offer you this day.
Let all my prayer, work, joy, suffering today
join with the lives offered to you
by the whole People of God
and especially with our great Eucharist,
Jesus,
your Son and our Brother.
Let your Spirit be with me today,
especially in . . .
And I ask your loving concern today,
especially for my friend . . .
Remind me, through the day, that I am not alone.
Amen.

Offering

DAYTIME

Presence | Living God,
my love of you ignites
only when I myself am the candle,
the fuel,
the consumed.

Grace: All right, God: I won't be perfect, but make me try.

Psalm | Love is patient, kind.
~~It is never jealous.~~
Love never boasts itself or puts on airs.
It is never rude or self-seeking,
always slow to take offense,
and holds no grudges after.
Love never feeds its self-esteem on others' weakness.
Love delights, instead, on doing truth.
Love's forbearance is tireless,
always ready to excuse,
to trust,
to hope,
to bear whatever comes.

(1 Corinthians 13:4–7)

Hymn | For Mercy has a human heart,
Pity a human face,
And Love, the human form divine,
And Peace, the human dress.

Then every man, of every clime,
That prays in his distress,
Prays to the human form divine,
Love, Mercy, Pity, Peace.

And all must love the human form,
In heathen, Turk, or Jew;
Where Mercy, Love, and Pity dwell
There God is dwelling too.

(William Blake, "The Divine Image")

The earth-mother can indeed take me now into the im-
mensity of her arms. She can enlarge me with her life, or
take me back into her primordial dust. She can adorn
herself for me with every allurement, every horror, every
mystery. She can intoxicate me with the scent of her tangi-
bility and her unity. She can throw me to my knees in
expectancy of what is maturing in her womb.

But all her enchantments can no longer harm me, since
she has become for me, more than herself and beyond herself, the body of him who is and who is to come.
(Pierre Teilhard de Chardin, *Hymn of the Universe*)

Out of his bottomless kindness, may God give you the
Holy Spirit, the power to make your hidden self be strong,
so that Christ may take root in the faith of your heart. And
then—rooted and grounded in loving—may you, with all
the other saints, be able to grasp the length and breadth,
the height and depth! Then, you will know the love of
Christ that is beyond all calculating knowledge, and you
will be filled with the utter fullness of God!
(Ephesians 3:16–19)

Loving God,
all right.
Again, I tell you I am not allowed perfection.
But love sounds too heart-stoppingly good
not to try.
Amen.

Reading

Scriptural Reading

Closing

EVENING

Presence | Living God,
you are not merely the provider,
you are the pathfinder.
Help me to store up provisions;
show me the paths.

Grace: Holy Spirit, keep who-I-am always under way.

Psalm 25 | God, shame is a gift I really never requested.
~~The sins of my youth, surely, I paid for long ago—~~
as if payment could expunge a slight to one like you.
If anything, I have been humble, aware of my hedging,
too aware, too aware—to the point of paralysis.
If the benighted are to find light,
let them open their eyes!
If the crippled will walk,
let them start with crawling!
If the fainthearted are to love,
let them first give trust.

Hymn | Yet all experience is an arch wherethrough
Gleams that untraveled world whose margin fades
Forever and forever when I move.
How dull it is to pause, to make an end,
To rust unburnished, not to shine in use!
As though to breathe were life! Life piled on life
Were all too little, and of one to me
Little remains; but every hour is saved
From that eternal silence, something more,
A bringer of new things; and vile it were
For some three suns to store and hoard myself,
And this grey spirit yearning in desire
To follow knowledge like a sinking star,
Beyond the utmost bound of human thought.
                              (Alfred Lord Tennyson, "Ulysses")

Holy Friend,
I'm truly tired.
You led me through the dance all week.
For tonight,
could we sit this last one out,
and merely be together?
Amen.

Closing

❧ Fourth Week ❧

Fourth Sunday

Presence | Living God,
today I will meet people ready-made.
Sharpen my senses to their susceptibilities.
Others have formed them and sent them to me.
Help me to send them on, enriched.

Grace: God, let me feel how privileged I am that others
try to work your will as well.

Psalm | Jesus said:
"My life, my food, my sustenance
is doing the will of the One who missions me,
to bring to fruition what God has begun.
When you plant, you say, 'Well, four months to harvest.'
But no. Look around you. Look to the fields.
When God sows, the harvest leaps to our hands.
In an instant! Full blown and ready for the reaper.
And the reaper follows the sower's footsteps, rejoicing.
God sows; God reaps. And we are God's hands.
I send you forth—you—to reap
fields tilled and broken and sown by others.
Your gift is the harvest. Then be on with it!"

(John 4:34–38)

Summer ends now; now, barbarous in beauty, the stooks[*] | **Hymn**
       arise
  Around; up above, what wind-walks! what lovely
       behaviour
Of silk-sack clouds! has wilder, wilful-wavier
Meal-drift moulded ever and melted across skies?

I walk, I lift up, I lift up heart, eyes,
  Down all that glory in the heavens to glean our
       Saviour;
  And, eyes, heart, what looks, what lips yet gave you a
Rapturous love's greeting of realer, of rounder replies?

And the azurous hung hills are his world-wielding shoulder
  Majestic—as a stallion stalwart, very-violet-sweet!—
These things, these things were here and but the beholder
  Wanting; which two when they once meet,
The heart rears wings bold and bolder
  And hurls for him, O half hurls earth for him off under
       his feet.
       (Gerard Manley Hopkins, "Hurrahing in Harvest")

God, my friend, | **Offering**
I offer you this day.
Let all my prayer, work, joy, suffering today
join with the lives offered to you
by the whole People of God
and especially with our great Eucharist,
Jesus,
your Son and our Brother.
Let your Spirit be with me today,
especially in . . .
And I ask your loving concern today,
especially for my friend . . .
Remind me, through the day, that I am not alone.
Amen.

[*]stooks=hayshocks

DAYTIME

Presence | Living God,
when Jesus was dogged by derision,
he withdrew into a noble silence
where he heard your approval drown out the mockery.
Draw me apart awhile
that I may share your confidence in me.

Grace: God, let my confidence and forgiveness bind our
community together.

Psalm | You—yes, you!—are God's chosen race of saints!
God's beloved! Then clothe yourself in Christ Jesus.
As a sign you have been chosen, wear a compassionate
heart,
kindness, humility, gentleness, patient endurance.
Bear one another's faults, one another's burdens.
While the quarrel still smolders, stop—and forgive.
Who are you—absolved—to withhold forgiveness?
Over all these clothes, to unify and complete them,
cloak your community in love—and be fulfilled.
Let the arbiter in your midst be the peace of Christ,
for it is his love that binds you into one Body.
For that peace, that harmony, be forever grateful.
(Colossians 3:12–15)

Hymn | He was fully sensible to the advantages of the Instalment
Plan
And had everything necessary to the Modern Man,
A phonograph, a radio, a car and a frigidaire.
Our researchers into Public Opinion are content
That he held the proper opinions for the time of year;
When there was peace, he was for peace; when there was
war, he went.
He was married and added five children to the population,
Which our Eugenist says was the right number for a parent
of his generation,
And our teachers report that he never interfered with their
education.
Was he free? Was he happy? The question is absurd:
Had anything been wrong, we should certainly have heard.
(W. H. Auden, "The Unknown Citizen")

What we suffer from to-day is humility in the wrong place. | **Reading**
Modesty has moved from the organ of ambition. Modesty
has settled upon the organ of conviction; where it was
never meant to be. A man was meant to be doubtful about
himself, but undoubting about the truth; this has been
exactly reversed. Nowadays the part of a man that a man
does assert is exactly the part he ought not to assert—
himself. The part he doubts is exactly the part he ought
not to doubt—the Divine Reason. . . . The truth is that
there is a real humility typical of our time; but it so hap-
pens that it is practically a more poisonous humility than
the wildest prostrations of the ascetic.

                (Gilbert K. Chesterton, *Orthodoxy*)

There is one feeling to which you are never to surrender: | **Scriptural**
fear of what others will say of you. For everything I have | **Reading**
told you in the silence of your heart, you must speak confidently in the full light of day. The stirrings of my Spirit in
your soul you must shout from the housetops. There is one
thing far worse than the death of your body: to go on living
with a soul that is already dead.

                      (Matthew 10:26–31)

Bountiful God, | **Closing**
more than a few find me a fool,
chuckle behind my back:
"Dreamer! Do-gooder! Pious fraud!"
What earthly need have I
for the approval of such small souls?
Help me to wipe them from my attention,
but not from my pity and forgiveness.
Amen.

EVENING

Presence

Living God,
even a day off goes by in a blur.
Let me focus myself in you—and you in me,
so that tomorrow I will be less opaque
to your clarity and peace.

Grace: God, help me put more forever into my todays.

Psalm

I AM
the bread of life.
Believe, and never hunger again,
nor ever thirst for more than me.
You see
but don't believe.
I've come to set you free
of yearning, bondage, rootlessness.
I've come to share with you
what God has given me:
the gift that I might do God's holy will.
I promise
that none of you
will ever truly die.
This new life I give you never ends.
Believe.

(John 6:35–40)

Hymn

I lift mine eyes, and all the windows blaze
    With forms of Saints and holy men who died,
    Here martyred and hereafter glorified;
    And the great Rose upon its leaves displays
Christ's Triumph, and the angelic roundelays,
    With splendor upon splendor multiplied;
    And Beatrice again at Dante's side
    No more rebukes, but smiles her words of praise.
And then the organ sounds, and unseen choirs
    Sing the old Latin hymns of peace and love
    And benedictions of the Holy Ghost;
And the melodious bells among the spires
    O'er all the house-tops and through heaven above
    Proclaim the elevation of the Host!
    (Henry Wadsworth Longfellow, "Divina Commedia")

Holy Friend,
you are my food
to knit up the fibers of my soul,
to heal the abraded feelings,
to becalm the frictions with forgiveness.
I rest in you.
Amen.

Closing

Fourth Monday

MORNING

Presence | Living God,
let me pause and catch your Spirit
so I will recognize you today
when you interrupt what I'd planned.

Grace: Always-present God, let me see you today where
no one else would have bothered to look.

Psalm | When the Son of Man comes in his glory
amid all the fiery presences of heaven,
he will ascend the throne he had surrendered for us,
and all humankind will be assembled there.
Then he will say to those at his right,
"Come, beloved of God. Welcome!
Take the heritage prepared for you
since long before there was space or time.
I was hungry and you fed me; you slaked my thirst.
I was outcast, but you drew me in, naked
but you clothed me, sick but not alone,
imprisoned, yet you visited me unashamed. . . .
I give my word: whenever you served
any of my loved ones whom the world dismissed,
you served me."

(Matthew 25:31–46)

Hymn | Thanks to St. Matthew, who had been
At mass-meetings in Palestine,
We knew whose side was spoken for
When Comrade Jesus had the floor.

"Where sore they toil and hard they lie,
Among the great unwashed, dwell I:—
The tramp, the convict, I am he;
Cold-shoulder him, cold-shoulder me."

(Sarah N. Cleghorn, "Comrade Jesus")

God, my friend,
I offer you this day.
Let all my prayer, work, joy, suffering today
join with the lives offered to you
by the whole People of God
and especially with our great Eucharist,
Jesus,
your Son and our Brother.
Let your Spirit be with me today,
especially in . . .
And I ask your loving concern today,
especially for my friend . . .
Remind me, through the day, that I am not alone.
Amen.

Offering

DAYTIME

Presence	Living God, I am no hireling. But I still feel the hireling's fears.
	Grace: God, let me own the truth: that halfway is not far enough.
Psalm	I am the true shepherd; appraise your life by mine. You know genuine shepherds by their willingness to risk, while hirelings endure the day, doing what they must. They have no heart for the sheep; their heart is in their purse. The sheep? When crisis comes, the hirelings cut and run; they are always aware of the cost to themselves. I am the good shepherd; appraise your life by mine. I read the shiverings of the sheep, and they know my voice, as God reads our heart and we bow to God. There are others, not of this fold, aliens to you, but they hear my voice, and they startle and stumble at your side, just as you did, yes, just as you.
	(John 10:11–16)
Hymn	Though much is taken, much abides; and though We are not now that strength which in old days Moved earth and heaven, that which we are, we are— One equal temper of heroic hearts, Made weak by time and fate, but strong in will To strive, to seek, to find, and not to yield.
	(Alfred Lord Tennyson, "Ulysses")

Reflect now, how Our Lord Himself spoke of Peace. He said to His disciples, "My peace I leave with you, my peace I give unto you." Did He mean peace as we think of it: the kingdom of England at peace with its neighbours, the barons at peace with the King, the householder counting over his peaceful gains, the swept hearth, his best wine for a friend at the table, his wife singing to the children? Those men His disciples knew no such things: they went forth to journey afar, to suffer by land and sea, to know torture, imprisonment, disappointment, to suffer death by martyrdom. What then did He mean? If you ask that, re-member then that He said also, "Not as the world gives, give I unto you." So then, He gave to His disciples peace, but not peace as the world gives.

(T. S. Eliot, *Murder in the Cathedral*)

Reading

The mother of the brothers stood, admirable and worthy of remembrance, watching, as her seven sons died on a single day, still holding fast to the one God of Israel. Her endur-ance was anchored in hope in the one God. Indeed, she urged them to their deaths in the language of their ances-tors. In her, the difference between woman and man had no meaning. "I have no way of knowing how you appeared in my womb," she said. "I did not squeeze the spirit of life into you. It was done within me, slowly shaping your every part. It was the Creator, who ordained the beginning of all—of the earth, of us—who gave you life, and who will surely give back your life and breath. Because you yield that life rather than yield your love of God—even if God's ways are inscrutable."

And the mother was the last to die, after her seven sons.

(2 Maccabees 7:20–41)

Scriptural Reading

God among us,
sometimes death seems easier
than the patient forbearance you ask.
Easier to die in the places of those I love
than to see them slip, so slowly, away.
Give me the humility to accept
that you have other plans for me.
Amen.

Closing

EVENING

Presence

Living God,
come into my soul and walk around the wounds
that I show to no one else but you.
Your Son was wounded, too.
And it failed to deter him.

Grace: God, let my memory of pain point me toward
others' pain.

Psalm

I thank Christ Jesus, my strength,
who judged me worthy to be chosen to serve,
even though I had proved my utter unworth.
But my very helplessness seduced his mercy,
and he filled my emptiness with trust and love.
Rely on this, then, the one, sure truth:
Christ Jesus came to the world for sinners.
And I the greatest—and thus the exemplar—
the final proof of his inexhaustible patience.
That was his purpose in ransoming me,
unworthy: to show what his mercy can do.
To the undying, invisible, and only God
be honor and glory forever. Amen.

(1 Timothy 1:12–17)

Hymn

Come down, O Christ, and help me! reach thy hand,
    For I am drowning in a stormier sea
    Than Simon on Thy lake of Galilee:
The wine of life is spilt upon the sand,
My heart is as some famine-murdered land,
    Whence all good things have perished utterly,
    And well I know my soul in Hell must lie
If I this night before God's throne should stand.
"He sleeps perchance, or rideth to the chase,
Like Baal, when his prophets howled that name
From morn to noon on Carmel's smitten height."
Nay, peace, I shall behold before the night,
    The feet of brass, the robe more white than flame,
    The wounded hands, the weary human face.

(Oscar Wilde, "E Tenebris")

Holy Friend,
It comes as no complete surprise to you
That I overdramatize myself,
seizing center stage,
monologuing about my never-ending need,
inflating my faults.
Let me settle back
to be a not newsworthy
and yet not unprofitable servant.
Amen.

Closing

Fourth Tuesday

MORNING

Presence | Living God,
remind me
that just as Jesus fused himself into human life,
he also fused our life into your life,
so that I am in you, and you are in me,
now.

Grace: Spirit of God, may your life-energy be embodied in
me today.

Psalm | He is the bodying-forth of the invisible God,
the firstborn of the never-ending creation.
Within him all heaven and earth were created:
all that is visible and invisible, without and within,
all things exist through him and for him.
Before anything came to be, he was,
and all things cohere together within him.
And we form one Body, with Christ as our head.
As he was the cause of life, he is the cause of rebirth,
the firstborn of the Resurrection as well,
for in all things, forever, he is first.
God willed all his fullness and wholeness in him,
that all fullness and wholeness might dwell in us,
so that humankind and all that is
might coalesce once again in God:
whole and holy, innocent and without blemish,
absorbed into Christ by his death on the cross.

(Colossians 1:15–20)

All, that he came to give,
He gave, and went again:
I have seen one man live,
I have seen one man reign,
With all the graces in his train. . . .
No man less proud than he,
Nor cared for homage less:
Only, he could not be
Far off from happiness:
Nature was bound to his success. . . .
Yet have I seen him live,
And owned my friend, a king:
All that he came to give,
He gave: and I, who sing
His praise, bring all I have to bring.

> (Lionel Johnson, "A Friend")

God, my friend,
I offer you this day.
Let all my prayer, work, joy, suffering today
join with the lives offered to you
by the whole People of God
and especially with our great Eucharist,
Jesus,
your Son and our Brother.
Let your Spirit be with me today,
especially in . . .
And I ask your loving concern today,
especially for my friend . . .
Remind me, through the day, that I am not alone.
Amen.

DAYTIME

Presence | Living God,
the world's ways wear me down.
The scheming, cunning, and callous seem to prevail.
Heal me of the heartlessness
I have caught from them.

Grace: God, give me the confidence to be vulnerable.

Psalm | God, your strength doesn't lie in numbers,
nor in the might and maneuvering of violent people,
for you are God of the humble; your power is peace.
You raise up the lowly, the downtrodden, the weak.
You embrace the forsaken and those who despair.
Please, God of my ancestors, please—
creator and ruler of earth and heaven—
hear the prayer of the daughter you have chosen.
Give me beguiling wits and words
when I stand before the powerful and cruel
who conspire against your peace, O God.
Let simplicity be my shrewdness.
Let openheartedness be my power.

(Judith 9:11–13)

Hymn | Drowning is not so pitiful
As the attempt to rise.
Three times, 'tis said, a sinking man
Comes up to face the skies,
And then declines forever
To that abhorred abode.
Where hope and he part company—
For he is grasped of God.
The Maker's cordial visage,
However good to see,
Is shunned, we must admit it,
Like an adversity.

(Emily Dickinson)

The evil to which even you should have referred was not suffering, but the unreasoning fear of suffering. *Metus doloris*. Take it together with its positive equivalent, the craving for worldly security, for Eden, and you might have your "root of evil.". . . To minimize suffering and to maximize security were natural and proper ends of society and Caesar. But then they became the only ends, somehow, and the only basis of law—a perversion. Inevitably, then, in seeking only them, we found only their opposites: maximum suffering and minimum security.

(Walter M. Miller, Jr., *A Canticle for Leibowitz*)

Reading

The word of God is alive, active. It cuts like a two-edged sword, but more finely. It can sense the soft junctures and slip through to the places where the joints are not fused to the bone, where the mind does not cleave to the soul.
It can penetrate to the secret thoughts of the mind and feelings of the heart, for nothing created is opaque to its Creator. Everything is naked to the eyes of God, to whom we must render account.

But Jesus, the Son of God, our high priest, is the anchor of our trust. He has shared all our weaknesses with us. He is one who was tempted, often, in every way we are, though he never relented. So then be confident in approaching the throne of grace. Since he knows our weakness and divisions, he knows our need—for which he has mercy and grace aplenty.

(Hebrews 4:12—5:13)

Scriptural Reading

Gracious God,
take away my fear
of being used,
of being out here all alone,
of being who you made me.
Amen.

Closing

EVENING

Presence | Living God,
I keep forgetting
who is in charge.
And until I do, I'll know no peace.
Help me remember.
Give me peace.

Grace: God, empty me of whatever gets in your way.

Psalm | God, you have seduced me
and—more the fool I!—
I let myself be duped,
Like some gullible, green child.
You overpowered my will;
you seized me and prevailed.
I am their laughingstock, their byword, their butt!
I tried to say, "No more!
I will not even think your name!"
But your word surges up in me
like a consuming fire, and I speak.
I am weary from trying to smother it,
and your fire bursts from me again.
There is no use to fighting your will.
You will have me. I am yours.

(Jeremiah 20:7–13)

Within my flowering breast
Which only for himself entire I save
He sank into his rest
And all my gifts I gave
Lulled by the airs with which the cedars wave.

Over the ramparts fanned
While the fresh wind was fluttering his tresses,
With his serenest hand
My neck he wounded, and
Suspended every sense with its caresses.

Lost to myself I stayed
My face upon my lover having laid
From all endeavour ceasing:
And all my cares releasing
Threw them amongst the lilies there to fade.
   (Saint John of the Cross, "Songs of the Soul in Rapture")

Holy Friend,
at times you ask too much.
Or so it seems.
Help me to realize—and believe—
that you know me
and love me
far better than I know and love myself.
Amen.

Fourth Wednesday

MORNING

Presence Living God,
there is a yearning in me for love—
by which, of course, I mean being loved.
But that hunger will rove restless and without relief
until I relent
and love.

Grace: Loving God, let me love—and let being loved
take care of itself.

Psalm Be at peace among yourselves.
If the community is to live as one,
you must have the courage to show your love:
warn the idlers of the needs of the weary;
give courage to the timid and apprehensive
and a shoulder to the weak; be patient with the strong.
You must never want to seek revenge,
but ponder what each and all need most.
Let your life be one of contagious joy,
enlivened by your times alone with God.
This is the life we share in Jesus the Christ.

(1 Thessalonians 5:14–18)

The dove descending breaks the air
With flame of incandescent terror
Of which the tongues declare
The one discharge from sin and error.
The only hope, or else despair
    Lies in the choice of pyre or pyre—
    to be redeemed from fire by fire.
Who then devised the torment? Love.
Love is the unfamiliar Name
Behind the hands that wove
The intolerable shirt of flame
Which human power cannot remove.
    We only live, only suspire
    Consumed by either fire or fire.
              (T. S. Eliot, "Little Gidding")

Hymn

God, my friend,
I offer you this day.
Let all my prayer, work, joy, suffering today
join with the lives offered to you
by the whole People of God
and especially with our great Eucharist,
Jesus,
your Son and our Brother.
Let your Spirit be with me today,
especially in . . .
And I ask your loving concern today,
especially for my friend . . .
Remind me, through the day, that I am not alone.
Amen.

Offering

DAYTIME

Presence

Living God,
let me break away awhile
from being knowledgeable, sophisticated, shrewd.
With you for these few moments,
I am your child,
and you are Abba.

Grace: Abba, keep me from taking myself too seriously.

Psalm

Let the learned not grow tiresome about their degrees,
nor the valiant wax eloquent about their lion's heart,
nor the wealthy boast of their palaces, paintings, power.
There is always One more listening than those they see.
If anyone cares to boast, let it be only this:
"My heart and mind and soul are at one with God;
the wisdom, the valor, the riches come from God,
who rules with integrity, justice, kindness."
I am the God of Israel. It is I who speak.

(Jeremiah 9:22–23)

Hymn

My period had come for Prayer—
No other Art—would do—
My Tactics missed a rudiment—
Creator—Was it you?

God grows above—so those who pray
Horizons—must ascend—
And so I stepped upon the North
To see this Curious Friend—

His house was not—no sign had He—
By Chimney—nor by Door
Could I infer his Residence—
Vast Prairies of Air

Unbroken by a Settler—
Were all that I could see—
Infinitude—Had'st Thou no Face
That I might look on Thee?

The Silence condescended—
Creation stopped—for Me—
But awed beyond my errand—
I worshipped—did not "pray"—

(Emily Dickinson)

Reading

Men (I felt) might fast forty days for the sake of hearing a blackbird sing. Men might go through fire to find a cowslip. Yet these lovers of beauty could not even keep sober for the blackbird. They would not go through common Christian marriage by way of recompense to the cowslip. Surely one might pay for extraordinary joy in ordinary morals. Oscar Wilde said that sunsets were not valued because we could not pay for sunsets. But Oscar Wilde was wrong; we can pay for sunsets. We can pay for them by not being Oscar Wilde.

(Gilbert K. Chesterton, *Orthodoxy*)

Scriptural Reading

They came to Capernaum, and when they had finally settled themselves in the house, Jesus looked around at his disciples and asked, "What were you arguing about as we were coming up the road?" They could not look at him or speak, because they had been arguing about who would be most important in this new Reign of God.

But Jesus knew their thoughts. Jesus beckoned for a small child to come to him. He embraced the child who rested on his knees. "See?" he said, "here is your answer. I give you my word, unless you change and become as open-hearted as little children, you will never even enter the Kingdom—much less be great in it."

(Mark 9:33–37)

Closing

God who is love,
what a great surprise it will be
when those who sneer and preen
and scowl at those of us who are clowns
finally see you face-to-face
and find it has been a circus all along.
Amen.

EVENING

Presence | Living God,
it is impossible to conceive of . . . nothing.
the utter cold and empty death-dark of it.
But if you were not here
in the secretmost part of me,
that is what I would truly be:
nothing.

Grace: God, give me a sense of you in this silence.

Psalm | Jesus said, "I tell you most solemnly,
unless you feed on my flesh and blood,
you will have no real life in you."
Many of those who listened were disturbed.
"Does that upset you?" Jesus asked.
"It is the Spirit who infuses life, not flesh.
These words I speak are the spirit of life."
And many turned and walked no more with him.
"And you," he said to the Twelve, "and you?
Will you turn away and leave me too?"
Peter said, "Jesus, to whom could we go
when you have the words that fulfill our life?"

(John 6:53–68)

Hymn | Where had I heard this wind before
Change like this to a deeper roar?
What would it take my standing there for,
Holding open a restive door,
Looking down hill to a frothy shore?
Summer was past and day was past.
Somber clouds in the west were massed.
Out in the porch's sagging floor,
Leaves got up in a coil and hissed,
Blindly struck at my knee and missed.
Something sinister in the tone
Told me my secret must be known:
Word I was in the house alone
Somehow must have gotten abroad,
Word I was in my life alone,
Word I had no one left but God.

(Robert Frost, "Bereft")

Holy Friend,
there is a place within me
no one can enter but you,
where I store my sometime shames,
my uncertainties,
my uncompleted self.
Come into that place and fill it.
Or I am barren.
Amen.

Closing

Fourth Thursday

MORNING

Presence Living God,
I am so spoiled,
so used to what you make
from what seems like nothing.
When people come back and tell me,
"I'll never forget when you said . . . ,"
and I cannot remember,
I know someone is at work besides myself.

Grace: God, let me leave to you where the good seed falls.

Psalm The angel came to her and said, "Peace, Mary.
Exalted one. Filled with grace. God is with you."
She was deeply disturbed by the angel's words and
          pondered.
But the angel said,
"Mary, do not be afraid. Listen!
You will conceive and bear a Son,
and the name he must bear is Jesus.
He will grow great, and he will be the Son of the Most
          High.
The one God will seat him on the throne of his forebear,
          David,
and his reign over his house will be forever and forever."
But Mary said, "But how shall this be? I know not man."
And the angel answered,
"The Spirit of God will overshadow you.
And the child you shall bear will be holy,
the Son of the Most High.
Know this, too: your aged kinswoman, Elizabeth,
is with child—
she whom all called barren—
for nothing is impossible to God."

And Mary said, "I am the handmaiden of our God.
If what you have said is God's desire,
it is my desire."

(Luke 1:26–38)

I sing of a maiden that is makeless;
King of all kings to her son she chose.
He came all so still there his mother was,
As dew in April that falleth on the grass. . . .
Mother and maiden was never none but she;
Well may such a lady God's mother be.

(Author unknown)

Hymn

God, my friend,
I offer you this day.
Let all my prayer, work, joy, suffering today
join with the lives offered to you
by the whole People of God
and especially with our great Eucharist,
Jesus,
your Son and our Brother.
Let your Spirit be with me today,
especially in . . .
And I ask your loving concern today,
especially for my friend . . .
Remind me, through the day, that I am not alone.
Amen.

Offering

DAYTIME

Presence Living God,
only fools ask for certitude, for surety, guarantees.
But, as I'm a fool, I crave them.
Cure me.

Grace: God, let me be unafraid of the wisdom that the
world spurns.

Psalm I shall not call you servants any more.
~~Servants do not know their master's mind.~~
Instead, I call you friends, because you know
that what the one God asks of me, God asks of you.
At times you feel you've really chosen me.
No. I chose you, the fruit of my love.
And now you must turn to seed and bear more fruit.
You, my chosen, will bear fruit to last forever,
and then our God will grant your every wish,
because you have lost your self in order to love.
(John 15:15–17)

Hymn Am I thy Gold? Or Purse, Lord, for thy Wealth;
    Whether in mine, or mint refinde for thee?
Ime counted so, but count me o're thyselfe,
    Lest gold washt face, and brass in Heart I bee.
    I Feare my Touchstone touches when I try
    Mee, and my Counted Gold too overly. . . .

Lord, make my Soule thy Plate: thine Image bright
    Within the Circle of the same enfoile.
And on its brims in golden Letters write
    Thy Superscription in an Holy style.
    Then I shall be thy Money, thou my Hord:
    Let me thy Angell bee, bee thou my Lord.
(Edward Taylor)

If we lived in a State where virtue was profitable, common sense would make us good, and greed would make us saintly. And we'd live like animals or angels in the happy land that *needs* no heroes. But since in fact we see that avarice, anger, envy, pride, sloth, lust and stupidity commonly profit far beyond humility, chastity, fortitude, justice and thought, and have to choose, to be human at all . . . why then perhaps we *must* stand fast a little—even at the risk of being heroes.

(Robert Bolt, *A Man for All Seasons*)

Reading

God said to Solomon, "Ask of me what you choose." But Solomon replied, "You showed great kindness to my father, David. But I am young, unskilled in leading. I am your servant, but this people is too numberless to reckon. Give your servant only a wise heart, to discern between good and evil, a mind to grasp the truth, and a will to see it through."

And God was pleased.

(1 Kings 3:5–10)

Scriptural Reading

God of mercy,
all day long we immerse ourselves in childish games:
one-upmanship.
pin-the-blame-on-the-donkey,
proving ourselves despite the odds.
Help me, finally, to grow up.
Amen.

Closing

EVENING

Presence

Living God,
all day long I've counted the cost.
The world I live in requires it of me.
But in the evermore we share,
gain is loss and loss is gain.
You made me to live in two contradictory lives,
and you lived it yourself.
You can understand my bewilderment.

Grace: ~~God, I lay my self on the table; take the dice.~~

Psalm

If any of you wants to come out on the road with me,
then leave your self behind. We go to the cross.
And not some day in the future, but today.
If you grasp what you have to lose, it is already lost.
But lay your heart at risk, and your heart is yours.
What profit to win the world, at the price of your self?

(Luke 9:23–26)

Hymn

Lord, when the sense of thy sweet grace
Sends up my soul to seek thy face,
Thy blessed eyes breed such desire,
I die in love's delicious Fire.
    O love, I am thy SACRIFICE.
Be still triumphant, blessed eyes.
Still shine on me, fair suns! that I
Still may behold, though still I die.

    Though still I die, I live again;
Still longing so to be still slain,
So gainfull is such losse of breath,
I die even in desire of death.
    Still live in me this loving strife
Of living DEATH & dying LIFE.
For while thou sweetly slayest me,
Dead to my selfe, I live in Thee.

(Richard Crashaw, "A Song")

Holy Friend,
I cannot remember this morning too well,
and not too much of today.
Perhaps that could be a sign
that I did what I could and then went on.
If that is true,
and I suspect it is,
I'm learning.
Amen.

Closing

Fourth Friday

Presence

Living God,
help me make peace with the tyrant, time.
It masters my thoughts,
slips through my fingers,
leaves me grinding my jaws,
which is not, I suspect, what you made it for.

Grace: God, let me be content with what one day allows
me.

Psalm 27

You, God, are the dawn of my day and my ransom.
With you as my shepherd, whom shall I fear?
No matter my shame, my head is held high,
for you have summoned me forth.
Your voice in my heart whispers, "Seek me."
Then, my God, don't hide your face from me.
And I trust. If my mother and father forsake me,
if my friends forget me and blot out my name,
my Savior is still at my side.

Teach me to feel another's woe,
    To hide the fault I see;
That mercy I to others show,
    That mercy show to me.

Mean though I am, not wholly so,
    Since quickened by thy breath;
Oh, lead me wheresoe'er I go,
    Through this day's life or death.

This day be bread and peace my lot:
    All else beneath the sun,
Thou know'st if best bestowed or not;
    And let Thy will be done.

To Thee, whose temple is all space,
    Whose altar, earth, sea, skies,
One chorus let all being raise;
    All nature's incense rise!
            (Alexander Pope, "The Universal Prayer")

Offering

God, my friend,
I offer you this day.
Let all my prayer, work, joy, suffering today
join with the lives offered to you
by the whole People of God
and especially with our great Eucharist,
Jesus,
your Son and our Brother.
Let your Spirit be with me today,
especially in . . .
And I ask your loving concern today,
especially for my friend . . .
Remind me, through the day, that I am not alone.
Amen.

DAYTIME

Presence | Living God,
I am part of the Body of your Son,
whose Body was blessed and then broken
and the pieces handed round
to feed the fainthearted,
to enliven the listless,
to multiply myself.
Then break me.

Grace: God, let me not be too frightened or too fragile.

Psalm | God has gifted us with one another.
Some are missioners, prophets, preachers of the News;
some are shepherds, and some teachers—
all of our gifts woven into one work:
to serve and build the Body of Christ.
Thus, we blend our gifts, our faith, our lives,
striving to form the perfect Son,
the same wholeness that lived in Jesus.
No longer, then, may we be children,
running about after this and then that,
ingenuous victims of tricks and deceits.
The spine of our Body is the truth of Christ,
the soul that impels it, our living love.
The head is Christ Jesus, melding and merging
each separate strength, each separate self,
into a single, growing self that serves.
And the gift that we were given, the gift we give,
is love.

(Ephesians 4:11–16)

Hear me, O God!
    A broken heart
    Is my best part:
Use still thy rod,
    That I may prove
    Therein, thy love.

If thou hadst not
    Been stern to me,
    But left me free,
I had forgot
    Myself and thee.
                (Ben Jonson, "An Hymn to God the Father")

"That there must be virtue in imperfection, for Man is imperfect, and Man is a creation of God.

"That there must be virtue in frailty, for Man is frail, and Man is a creation of God.

"That there must be virtue in inefficiency, for Man is inefficient, and Man is a creation of God.

"That there must be virtue in brilliance followed by stupidity, for Man is alternately brilliant and stupid, and Man is a creation of God."
                (Kurt Vonnegut, Jr., *Player Piano*)

Jesus told them another parable. "The Reign of God is like a mustard seed that a farmer took and sowed in a field. It is the tiniest and most insignificant of seeds, and yet it grows, slowly toiling upward and swelling into a strong tree. And the birds of the air come and find shelter in its branches."
                (Matthew 13:31–32)

Holy God,
some people find me
an actual obstacle to finding you.
Remind me that you have others to welcome them,
with more than enough left for me.
Amen.

EVENING

Presence

Living God,
all day I walk cocooned in a little world
in which the problems and pains—and I—
all balloon out of size,
cramping the tiny, airless space.
Crack open my cocoon,
and let me feel the endless depths of real space.
Let me rejoice in my smallness.

Grace: God, let me know that my being is important, but
that only yours is essential.

Psalm 148

Let the heavens proclaim you, Holy One—
the songs of the angels in the depths of space,
the great carouse of the planets and stars!
Praise God at whose command we became!
Let the whole motley, harlequin earth
leap with joy and sing praise!
We thunder your name and echo it round
the snow-caped heights and shadowed canyons.
Let the fields glorify God with growing,
the birds with soaring, and foals with leaping.
Young boys and girls, old crones and cronies,
babes at the breast—shout to the skies!
For you, God, are life among us—
and we are alive!

Hymn

Lead, kindly Light, amid the encircling gloom;
    Lead thou me on!
The night is dark, and I am far from home;
    Lead thou me on!
Keep thou my feet: I do not ask to see
The distant scene; one step enough for me. . . .
So long thy power hath blest me, sure it still
    Will lead me on,
O'er moor and fen, o'er crag and torrent, till
    The night is gone;
And with the morn, those angel faces smile
Which I have loved long since, and lost awhile.
        (John Henry Newman, "The Pillar of the Cloud")

Holy Friend,
I let go of the day in peace.
My mind is littered with unfinished business.
But then, so is yours.
If I don't get to it, you will.
But I would be grateful for another tomorrow.
Amen.

Closing

Fourth Saturday

MORNING

Presence Living God,
at times—not always, but at times—
I'm dulled to the signals you send me.
It's the rasp of pain that shocks me awake.
If that's what I need,
use that.

       Grace: God, despite my reluctance, remind me that there
                   is a great deal of me that we have not yet used.

Psalm "The reason I teach you in stories," Jesus said,
"is that your eyes are open but sightless, dead.
Your ears prick up and hear only silence.
You listen and listen, and understand nothing;
you peer about, and peer, but never perceive.
For your heart is tough as a tightened fist,
your ears echo like empty shells,
your eyes clamp shut for fear of what you will see.
Open! Hear! See! Me."

                                        (Matthew 13:14–17)

Hymn Lord, what am I, that, with unceasing care,
Thou didst seek after me,—that Thou didst wait,
Wet with unhealthy dews, before my gate,
And pass the gloomy nights of winter there?

O, strange delusion, that I did not greet
Thy blest approach! and, O, to heaven how lost,
If my ingratitude's unkindly frost
Has chilled the bleeding wounds upon Thy feet!
How oft my guardian angel gently cried,
"Soul, from thy casement look, and thou shalt see
How he persists to knock and wait for thee!"
And O, how often to that voice of sorrow,
"To-morrow we will open," I replied!
And when the morrow came I answered still,
    "To-morrow."

(Lope de Vega, "To-morrow")

Offering

God, my friend,
I offer you this day.
Let all my prayer, work, joy, suffering today
join with the lives offered to you
by the whole People of God
and especially with our great Eucharist,
Jesus,
your Son and our Brother.
Let your Spirit be with me today,
especially in . . .
And I ask your loving concern today,
especially for my friend . . .
Remind me, through the day, that I am not alone.
Amen.

🌞

DAYTIME

Presence

Living God,
heaven is around and within me.
I sense it,
as the blind sense shape with their fingers.
Let me pause and sense the eternity in me.

Grace: God, let the chance to love be its own
        recompense.

Psalm | Love will be without reserve in us
when we can face the Judgment Day, forswearing fear,
because even here on earth we loved as God loves.
All fear will melt away in the face of love,
for fear expects rejection for its faults,
and those who fear forgiveness forfeit love.
We love, not because we're worthy, but because we're
    loved.
Those who bragged about their great love of God—
but hated or ignored their sisters and brothers—
are liars.
If they cannot love those they are able to see,
how can they love God, whom no one has ever seen?
So this is the commandment that Love has given us:
to love your God, you first must love one another.

(1 John 4:17–21)

Hymn | Give us
A pure heart
That we may see Thee,
A humble heart
That we may hear Thee,
A heart of love
That we may serve Thee,
A heart of faith
That we may live Thee,

Thou
Whom I do not know
But Whose I am.
Thou
Whom I do not comprehend
But Who hast dedicated me
To my fate.
Thou—

(Dag Hammarskjöld, *Markings*)

Because children have abounding vitality, because they are in spirit fierce and free, therefore they want things repeated and unchanged. They always say, "Do it again"; and the grown-up person does it again until he is nearly dead. For grown-up people are not strong enough to exult in monotony. . . . It is possible that God says every morning, "Do it again" to the sun; and every evening, "Do it again" to the moon. . . . It may be that He has the eternal appetite of infancy; for we have sinned and grown old, and our Father is younger than we.

(Gilbert K. Chesterton, Orthodoxy)

Reading

You are the heirs of God! But even if you have your inheritance put right into your hands, you are no more than slaves for as long as you remain as fearful as children, enslaved to bogies and suppressions and taboos. You remain tied to guardians and administrators until they tell you the time has come when you may come of age. Don't you realize that that time has already come! God sent Jesus the Christ, born of a woman as we were—subject to the Law, but sent to *ransom* us from enslavement to the Law—to enable us to be adopted as God's daughters and sons. The proof that you are sons and daughters is the God-sent Spirit who cries out from our heart, "Abba!"

    You are not slaves any more! You are God's children, the heirs through Christ of God's Kingdom!

(Galatians 4:1–7)

Scriptural Reading

God with us,
younger and wiser and freer than I,
time has never taught you
caution or counting the cost,
the weary surrender to safe routine,
the shrewd art of withdrawal to silence.
Infuse me with your enthusiasm;
thwart my artful dodging with your love.
Amen.

Closing

EVENING

Presence | Living God,
I've carried you through the day,
most often as unaware
as I was of the light in this room.
No matter.
So long as there is more light
than before we passed through.

Grace: God, let whatever I've known of darkness help
others toward the light.

Psalm 71 | You alone are my hope, O God.
Since you spun my flesh in my mother's womb,
since you drew me forth into light and air,
since my youth—you are the one unflinching star.
And now that I am older and somewhat wise,
there is still no other truth than you.
Let my life and love be a hymn of praise
to you who knew me before my birth.
But more.
Let the joy of my days be a snare for the young;
let me lure them from lackluster lives to Life;
let my love and patience entice them to you.

Hymn | Amazing grace! How sweet the sound
That saved a wretch like me!
I once was lost, but now am found,
Was blind but now I see. . . .
Through many dangers, toils, and snares
I have already come;
'Tis grace has brought me safe thus far,
And grace will lead me home. . . .
When we've been there ten thousand years,
Bright shining as the sun,
We've no less days to sing God's praise
Than when we first begun.

(John Newton, "Amazing Grace")

Holy Friend,
let me remember all my days,
that anything you have had me surrender
will return
full measure,
pressed down,
shaken together,
and running over.
Amen.

Closing

Acknowledgments (*continued*)

The poem by Gerard Manley Hopkins on page 13 is from *Poems of Gerard Manley Hopkins*, 3d ed., edited by W. H. Gardner (New York and London: Oxford University Press, 1948), page 70.

The excerpt on page 14 is from *The Merchant of Venice*, by William Shakespeare, reprinted in *Familiar Quotations*, by John Bartlett, 15th ed., edited by Emily Morison Beck (Boston: Little, Brown and Co., 1980), page 200.

The excerpt on page 15 is adapted from *The Trial of St. Thomas More*, by E. E. Reynolds (New York: P. J. Kenedy and Sons, 1964), pages 131–132. Copyright © 1964 by E. E. Reynolds. Used with permission of Burns and Oates.

The excerpt from the poem by George Herbert on page 16 is from *The Works of George Herbert*, edited by F. E. Hutchinson (London: Oxford University Press, 1941), page 92.

The poem by John Donne on pages 18–19 is from *The Complete Poetry and Selected Prose of John Donne*, edited by Charles M. Coffin (New York: Random House, 1952), page 252.

The poem by William Shakespeare on page 20 is from *The Norton Anthology of English Literature*, 4th ed., edited by M. H. Abrams (New York and London: W. W. Norton and Co., 1979), page 804.

The excerpt on page 21 is from *The Brothers Karamazov*, by Fyodor Dostoyevsky, translated by David Magarshack (Baltimore: Penguin Books, 1958), page 375. Copyright 1958 by David Magarshack.

The excerpt from the poem by T. S. Eliot on page 22 is from *Collected Poems 1909–1962*, by T. S. Eliot (Orlando, FL: Harcourt Brace Jovanovich and Faber and Faber), pages 1068–1069. Copyright 1936 by Harcourt Brace Jovanovich; copyright © 1963, 1964 by T. S. Eliot. Reprinted by permission of Harcourt Brace Jovanovich and Faber and Faber.

The poem by Gerard Manley Hopkins on pages 24–25 is from *Poems of Gerard Manley Hopkins*, edited by Gardner, page 73.

The excerpt from the poem by Robert Frost on page 26 is from *The Poetry of Robert Frost*, edited by Edward Connery Lathem (New York: Henry Holt and Co., 1949). Copyright © 1951, © 1956, 1958 by Robert Frost. Copyright © 1967 by Lesley Frost Ballantine. Reprinted by permission of Henry Holt and Co. and Johnathan Cape.

The excerpt on page 27 is from *Making Sense Out of Suffering*, by Peter Kreeft (Servant Publications, P.O. Box 8617, Ann Arbor, MI 48107, 1986), page 133. Copyright © 1986 by Peter Kreeft. Used with permission of the publisher.

The excerpt from the poem by Francis Thompson on page 29 is from *Complete Poems of Francis Thompson* (New York: Random House, n.d.), pages 88–93.

The second excerpt on page 29 is from *Markings*, by Dag Hammarskjöld, translated by Leif Sjöberg and W. H. Auden (New York: Ballantine Books, 1983), page 89. Translation copyright © 1964 by Alfred A. Knopf and Faber and Faber. Reprinted by permission of Random House and Faber and Faber.

The excerpt from the poem by John Masefield on page 31 is from *Poems*, by John Masefield (New York: Macmillan Co., 1962), pages 53–54. Copyright © 1951 by John Masefield. Used with permission of the Society of Authors as the literary representative of the estate of John Masefield.

The poem by e.e. cummings on page 32 is reprinted from *IS 5 poems*, by e. e. cummings, edited by George James Firmage (New York: Harcourt, Brace and World, 1954). Copyright © 1985 by E. E. Cummings Trust. Copyright © 1926 by Horace Liveright. Copyright © 1954 by e. e. cummings. Copyright © 1985 by George James Firmage. Used by permission of Liveright Publishing Corp. and Grafton Books, a division of Harper Collins Publishers.

The excerpt on page 33 is from *The Power and the Glory*, by Graham Greene (New York: Viking Press, 1940), pages 268–269. Copyright © 1940 by Graham Greene. Used by permission of Viking Penguin, a division of Penguin USA.

The poem by e.e. cummings on page 35 is reprinted from *Complete Poems, 1913–1962*, by e. e. cummings (New York: Harcourt, Brace and World, 1958), page 77. Copyright © 1923, 1925, 1931, 1935, 1938, 1940, 1944, 1945, 1946, 1947, 1948, 1949, 1950, 1951, 1952, 1953, 1954, 1955, 1956, 1957, 1958, 1959, 1960, 1961, 1962 by the trustees for the E. E. Cummings Trust. Copyright © 1961, 1963, 1968 by Marion Morehouse Cummings. Used by permission of Liveright Publishing Corp. and Grafton Books, a division of Harper Collins Publishers.

The poem by e.e. cummings on page 37 is reprinted from *XAIPE*, by e. e. cummings, edited by George James Firmage (New York: Harcourt, Brace and World, 1954). Copyright © 1950 by e. e. cummings. Copyright © 1973, 1978, 1979 by Nancy T. Andrews. Copyright © 1973, 1979 by George James Firmage. Used by permission of Liveright Publishing Corp. and Grafton Books, a division of Harper Collins Publishers.

The excerpt beginning on page 38 is from *The Poetic and Dramatic Works of Alfred Lord Tennyson* (Boston: Houghton Mifflin Co., n.d.), page 89.

The second excerpt on page 39 is from *Hymn of the Universe*, by Pierre Teilhard de Chardin (New York: Harper and Row, Publishers, 1969), page 21. Copyright © 1961 by Editions du Seuil, English translation © 1965 by William Collins Sons and Co., London, and Harper and Row, Publishers, New York. Reprinted by permission of the publisher.

The poem by William Wordsworth on page 40 is from *The Poetical Works of Wordsworth*, edited by Thomas Hutchinson, revised by Ernest de Selincourt (London: Oxford University Press, 1936), page 205.

The poem by Ben Jonson on page 43 is from *Masterpieces of Religious Verse*, edited by James Dalton Morrison (New York: Harper and Row, Publishers, 1948), page 364.

The poem by Robert Frost on page 44 is from *The Poetry of Robert Frost*. Reprinted by permission of Henry Holt and Co. and Johnathan Cape.

The excerpt on page 45 is from *The Man on a Donkey*, by H. F. M. Prescott (New York: Macmillan Co., 1952), page 517. Copyright © 1952 by H. F. M. Prescott; copyright renewed © 1980 by Patrick Downey. Reprinted with permission of Macmillan Publishing Co. and A. P. Watt on behalf of J. W. Prescott and Mrs. S. C. Thedinga.

The poem by Gerard Manley Hopkins on page 47 is from *Poems of Gerard Manley Hopkins*, edited by Gardner, page 113.

The poem by George Herbert on page 49 is from *The Works of George Herbert*, edited by Hutchinson, pages 62–63.

The song lyric on pages 50–51 is adapted from "Battle-Hymn of the Republic," composed by Julia Ward Howe (1819–1910).

The second excerpt on pages 50–51 is from *Mere Christianity*, by C. S. Lewis (New York: Collier Books, Macmillan Publishing Co., 1952), page 187. Copyright © 1943, 1945, 1952 by Macmillan Publishing Co. Used by permission of Collins Publishers, London.

The poem by John Donne on page 52 is from *The Complete Poetry and Selected Prose of John Donne*, edited by Coffin, pages 270–271.

The poem by George Herbert on page 57 is from *The Works of George Herbert*, edited by Hutchinson, pages 159–160.

The poem by Rainer Maria Rilke on page 58 is from *Translations from the Poetry of Rainer Maria Rilke*, by M. D. Herter Norton (New York: W. W. Norton and Co., 1938), page 75. Copyright © 1938 by W. W. Norton and Co. Copyright renewed © 1966 by M. D. Herter Norton. Used by permission of the publisher.

The excerpt from the poem by William Cullen Bryant on page 61 is from *Poems of William Cullen Bryant* (New York: A. L. Burt Co., n.d.), pages 294–295.

The poem by John Milton on pages 62–63 is from *Complete Poetry and Selected Prose of John Milton* (New York: Random House, n.d.), page 86.

The poem by George Herbert on page 64 is from *The Works of George Herbert*, edited by Hutchinson, page 189.

The excerpt on page 65 is from *New Seeds of Contemplation*, by Thomas Merton (New York: Dell Publishing Co., 1949). Copyright 1961 by Our Lady of Gethsemani. Reprinted by permission of New Directions Publishing Corp., New York, and Anthony Clarke, Wheathampstead, England.

The poem by Gilbert K. Chesterton on page 66 is from *A G. K. Chesterton Anthology*, selected and with an introduction by P. J. Kavanagh (San Francisco: Ignatius Press), page 1. Copyright © 1985 Miss D. E. Collins. Reprinted by permission of the publisher.

The poem by Walt Whitman on page 69 is from *The American Tradition in Literature*, vol. 2, 6th ed., edited by George Perkins, et al. (New York: Random House, 1985), page 106.

The excerpt from the poem by John Donne on page 70 is from *The Complete Poetry and Selected Prose of John Donne*, edited by Coffin, pages 271–272.

The excerpt on page 71 is from *Markings*, by Hammarskjöld, page 9. Reprinted by permission of the publisher.

The excerpt from the poem by James Russell Lowell on page 72 is from *The Complete Poetical Works of James Russell Lowell* (Boston: Houghton Mifflin Co., n.d.), page 107.

The poem on page 74 is from *Collected Poems*, by Vachel Lindsay (New York: Macmillan Co., 1926), page 69.

The poem by William Cowper on page 76 is from *Cowper: Poetical Works*, 4th ed., edited by H. S. Milford with corrections and additions by Norma Russell (London: Oxford University Press, 1967), page 455.

The excerpt on page 77 is from a speech of Albert Einstein's as it appears in the essay *The Myth of Simplicity*, by Yehuda Elkana, from *Albert Einstein: Historical and Cultural Perspectives*, edited by Gerald Holton and Yehuda Elkana (Princeton, NJ: Princeton University Press, 1982), page 240.

The poem by Robert Frost on page 79 is from *The Poetry of Robert Frost*. Reprinted by permission of Henry Holt and Co. and Johnathan Cape.

The excerpt from the poem by T. S. Eliot on page 81 is from *Collected Poems 1909–1962*, pages 1182–1183. Reprinted by permission of Harcourt Brace Jovanovich and Faber and Faber.

The excerpt from the poem by John Donne on page 82 is from *The Complete Poetry and Prose of John Donne*, edited by Coffin, page 252.

The excerpt on page 83 is from *St. Francis of Assisi: Writings and Early Biographies*, edited by Marion A. Habig (Chicago: Franciscan Herald Press, 1973), page 110. Copyright © 1973 by Franciscan Herald Press. Used with permission.

The poem by George Herbert on page 84 is from *The Works of George Herbert*, edited by Hutchinson, pages 132–133.

The poem by Elinor Wylie on page 87 is from *Collected Poems of Elinor Wylie* (New York: Alfred A. Knopf, 1931), page 187. Copyright © 1932 by Alfred A. Knopf and renewed © 1960 by Edwina C. Rubenstein. Reprinted by permission of the publisher.

The poem by Edwin Arlington Robinson on page 88 is from *Selected Poems of Edwin Arlington Robinson*, edited by Morton Dauwen Zabel (New York: Collier Books, 1966), pages 10–11.

The excerpt on page 89 is from *The End of the Affair*, by Graham Greene (New York: Viking Press, 1951), page 147. Copyright © 1951 by Graham Greene. Used by permission of Viking Penguin, a division of Penguin USA.

The poem by Emily Dickinson on page 91 is from *The Complete Poems of Emily Dickinson*, edited by Thomas H. Johnson, Cambridge, Mass. (Boston: Little, Brown and Co., 1960; the Belknap Press of Harvard University Press), page 350. Copyright © 1929 by Martha Dickinson Bianchi; renewed © 1957 by Mary L. Hampson; Copyright © 1951, 1979, 1983 by the President and Fellows of Harvard College. Used by permission of Little, Brown and Co. and the publishers and the trustees of Amherst College.

The excerpt from the poem by Arthur Hugh Clough on page 93 is from *The Poems of Arthur Hugh Clough*, edited by A. L. P. Norrington (London: Oxford University Press, 1968), pages 60–61.

The poem by Henry Vaughan on page 94 is from *The Higher Life* (Scholarly Press, 1972), page 343.

The excerpt on page 95 is from *The Intellectual Life: Its Spirit, Conditions, Methods*, by A. D. Sertillanges (Westminster, MD: Newman Press, 1948), page 165.

The excerpt from the poem by Thomas Hardy on page 96 is from *Collected Poems of Thomas Hardy* (New York: Macmillan Co., 1926), page 137.

The poem by Robert Graves on page 101 is from *Robert Graves Collected Poems 1975* (Garden City, NY: Doubleday and Co., 1961). Copyright © 1958, 1961 by Co-Productions Roterman S.A. Copyright © 1975 by Robert Graves. Used with permission of Oxford University Press, Inc., and A. P. Watt on behalf of the trust of the Robert Graves Copyright Trust.

The excerpt from the poem by Alfred Lord Tennyson on page 102 is from *The Poetic and Dramatic Works of Alfred Lord Tennyson*, page 175.

The excerpt on page 103 is from *Mere Christianity*, by Lewis, page 181. Used by permission of Collins Publishers, London.

The excerpt from the poem by George Herbert on page 104 is from *The Higher Life*, page 283.

The excerpt from the poem by W. H. Auden on page 106 is from *The Collected Poetry of W. H. Auden*, edited by Edward Mendelson (New York: Random House, 1945), page 143. Copyright © 1940 by W. H. Auden. Used by permission of Random House and Faber and Faber.

The poem by Percy Bysshe Shelley on page 108 is from *The Complete Poetical Works of Percy Bysshe Shelley* (London: Oxford University Press, 1905), page 550.

The second excerpt on page 108 is from *Helena*, by Evelyn Waugh (Boston: Little, Brown and Co., 1950). Copyright 1950 by Evelyn Waugh. Used with permission.

The poem on page 110 is from *Sacred Poems*, by Henry Vaughan (London: G. Bell and Sons, 1914), page 70.

The excerpt from the poem by John Milton on page 113 is from *Complete Poetry and Selected Prose of John Milton*, pages 9–10.

The excerpt from the poem by e.e. cummings on pages 114–115 is reprinted from *XAIPE*, by cummings. Used by permission of Liveright Publishing Corp. and Grafton Books, a division of Harper Collins Publishers.

The excerpt on page 115 is from *Walking on Water: Reflections on Faith and Art*, by Madeleine L'Engle (Wheaton, IL: Harold Shaw Publishers), page 193. Copyright © 1980 by Crosswicks.

The excerpt from the poem by Ezra Pound on page 117 is from *Ezra Pound: Personae* (New York: New Directions Publishing Corp., 1976), page 113. Copyright © 1926 by Ezra Pound. Reprinted by permission of New Directions Publishing Corp. and Faber and Faber.

The excerpt from the poem by Christina Georgina Rossetti on page 119 is from *The Poetical Works of Christina Georgina Rossetti* (London: Macmillan and Co., 1935), pages 60–61.

The poems by Gerard Manley Hopkins on pages 123 and 126 are from *Poems of Gerard Manley Hopkins*, edited by Gardner, pages 70–71.

The song lyric on page 124 is from "Morning Has Broken," composed by Eleanor Farjeon. Reprinted by permission of Harold Ober Associates and Oxford University Press. Copyright © 1957 by Eleanor Farjeon.

The excerpt on page 127 is from *The Diary of a Country Priest*, by Georges Bernanos. Translated from the French by Pamela Morris (New York: Macmillan Co., 1937), page 253. Copyright © 1937 by Macmillan Publishing Co., renewed © 1965. Reprinted by permission of the publisher.

The poem by D. H. Lawrence on page 128 is from *The Complete Poems of D. H. Lawrence*, edited by Vivian de Sola Pinto and Warren Roberts (Harmondsworth, Middlesex, England: Penguin Books, 1977), pages 726–727. Copyright © 1964, 1971 by Angelo Ravagli and C. M. Weekley, executors of the estate of Frieda Lawrence Ravagli. Used by permission of Viking Penguin, a division of Penguin USA.

The excerpt from the poem by Edward Taylor on page 131 is from *The Poems of Edward Taylor*, edited by Donald E. Stanford (New Haven, CT: Yale University Press, 1960), page 387. Copyright © 1960, renewed © 1988 by Donald E. Stanford. Used with permission.

The excerpt from the poem by George Herbert on page 132 is from *The Works of George Herbert*, edited by Hutchinson, page 43.

The excerpt on page 133 is from *Mere Christianity*, by Lewis, page 167. Used by permission of Collins Publishers, London.

The excerpt from the poem by Alexander Pope on page 134 is from *The Poetical Works of Alexander Pope* (New York: A. L. Burt Co., n.d.), page 222.

The poem by Richard Realf on page 136 is from *Masterpieces of Religious Verse*, edited by Morrison, page 6.

The excerpt from the poem by William Blake on page 138 is from *The Poetical Works of William Blake*, edited by John Sampson (London: Oxford University Press, 1913), page 5.

The excerpt on page 139 is from *Hymn of the Universe*, by Teilhard de Chardin, pages 142–143. Reprinted by permission of the publisher.

The excerpt from the poem by Alfred Lord Tennyson on page 140 is from *Immortal Poems of the English Language*, edited by Oscar Williams (New York: Washington Square Press, n.d.), page 376.

The poem by Gerard Manley Hopkins on page 145 is from *Poems of Gerard Manley Hopkins*, edited by Gardner, pages 74–75.

The excerpt from the poem by W. H. Auden on page 146 is from *The Collected Poetry of W. H. Auden*, edited by Edward Mendelson (New York: Random House, 1945), page 143. Copyright © 1940 by W. H. Auden. Used by permission of the publisher.

The excerpt on page 147 is from *Orthodoxy*, by Gilbert K. Chesterton (Garden City, NY: Doubleday and Co., 1959), page 31.

The excerpt from the poem by Henry Wadsworth Longfellow on page 148 is from *The American Tradition in Literature*, 5th ed., edited by Sculley Bradley, et al. (New York: Random House, 1985), page 1501.

The excerpt from the poem by Sarah N. Cleghorn on page 150 is from *Masterpieces of Religious Verse*, edited by Morrison, page 473.

The excerpt from the poem by Alfred Lord Tennyson on page 152 is from *Immortal Poems of the English Language*, edited by Williams, page 377.

The excerpt on page 153 is from *Murder in the Cathedral*, by T. S. Eliot (Orlando, FL: Harcourt Brace Jovanovich and Faber and Faber), page 48. Copyright 1935 by Harcourt Brace Jovanovich and renewed 1963 by T. S. Eliot. Reprinted by permission of Harcourt Brace Jovanovich and Faber and Faber.

The poem by Oscar Wilde on page 154 is from *The Works of Oscar Wilde: Poems* (New York: Lamb Publishing Co., 1909), page 94.

The excerpt from the poem by Lionel Johnson on page 157 is from *Poetical Works of Lionel Johnson* (New York: Macmillan Co., 1915), pages 11–12.

The poem by Emily Dickinson on page 158 is from *The Complete Poems of Emily Dickinson*, edited by Johnson, page 698.

The excerpt on page 159 is from *A Canticle for Leibowitz*, by Walter M. Miller, Jr. (New York: Bantam Books, 1959), page 305. Copyright 1959 by Walter M. Miller, Jr.

The poem by Saint John of the Cross on page 161 is from *The Poems of St. John of the Cross*, translated by Roy Campbell (New York: Pantheon Books, 1951), page 13. Used by permission of Burns and Oates, England.

The excerpt from the poem by T. S. Eliot on page 163 is from *Four Quartets*, by T. S. Eliot (New York: Harcourt Brace Jovanovich and Faber and Faber, 1943), pages 37–38. Copyright 1943 by T. S. Eliot and renewed 1971 by Esme Valerie Eliot. Reprinted by permission of Harcourt Brace Jovanovich and Faber and Faber.

The poem by Emily Dickinson on pages 164–165 is from *The Complete Poems of Emily Dickinson*, edited by Johnson, pages 274–275. Used by permission of Little, Brown and Co. and the publishers and the trustees of Amherst College.

The excerpt on page 165 is from *Orthodoxy*, by Chesterton, page 58.

The poem by Robert Frost on page 166 is from *The Poetry of Robert Frost*. Reprinted by permission of Henry Holt and Co. and Johnathan Cape.

The poem by Edward Taylor on page 170 is from *The Poems of Edward Taylor*, edited by Stanford, page 16. Used with permission.

The excerpt on page 171 is from *A Man for All Seasons*, by Robert Bolt (New York: Vintage Books, a division of Random House), page 81. Copyright © 1960, 1962 by Robert Bolt. Used with permission.

The poem by Richard Crashaw on page 172 is adapted from *The Poems of Richard Crashaw*, 2d ed., edited by L. C. Martin (Oxford: Clarendon Press, 1927), page 327.

The excerpt from the poem by Alexander Pope on page 175 is from *The Poetical Works of Alexander Pope*, page 222.

The excerpt from the poem by Ben Jonson on page 177 is from *The Works of Ben Jonson*, vol. 8 (London: G. and W. Nicol, et al., 1816), page 299.

The second excerpt on page 177 is from *Player Piano*, by Kurt Vonnegut, Jr. (New York: Dell Publishing Co., 1951), page 262. Copyright © 1952 by Kurt Vonnegut, Jr.

The poem by John Henry Newman on page 178 is from *Masterpieces of Religious Verse*, edited by Morrison, page 89.

The poem by Lope de Vega on pages 180–181 is from *The Higher Life*, page 94.

The excerpt on page 182 is from *Markings*, by Hammarskjöld, page 189. Reprinted by permission of the publisher.

The excerpt on page 183 is from *Orthodoxy*, by Chesterton, page 60.

The song lyric on page 184 is from "Amazing Grace," verses 1–4 composed by John Newton (1725–1807).